DESIGN & VISUAL IDENTITY

FOR CHILDREN'S SPACES

DESIGN & VISUAL IDENTITY

FOR CHILDREN'S SPACES

images
Publishing

Published in Australia in 2021 by
The Images Publishing Group Pty Ltd
ABN 89 059 734 431

Offices

Melbourne
6 Bastow Place
Mulgrave, Victoria 3170
Australia
Tel: +61 3 9561 5544

New York
6 West 18th Street 4B
New York, NY 10011
United States
Tel: +1 212 645 1111

Shanghai
6F, Building C, 838 Guangji Road
Hongkou District, Shanghai 200434
China
Tel: +86 021 31260822

books@imagespublishing.com
www.imagespublishing.com

The Images Publishing Group Reference Number: 1571

NATIONAL LIBRARY OF AUSTRALIA

A catalogue record for this book is available from the National Library of Australia

Title: Design & Visual Identity for Children's Spaces
Author: Carlos Martínez Trujillo (Introduction)
ISBN: 9781864708813

Printed by Everbest Printing Investment Limited, in Hong Kong/China

IMAGES has included on its website a page for special notices in relation to this and its other publications.
Please visit www.imagespublishing.com

Contents

Introduction

Written by Carlos Martínez Trujillo, Founder and Principal of BIENAL

Carlos Martínez Trujillo is the founder and principal of BIENAL, an art, design, and narrative studio specialized in the creation of concepts and brands that have won multiple awards internationally. As a visual communicator, Carlos' visual eclecticism is highly instinctual and individualistic, combining his formal education with his experimental and self-taught ideas. His passion for exploring turned him into an artifact and object collector, amassing pieces characterized by the presence of design, history, craftsmanship, and "soul." His work is prominent, displaying the mark of his travels and his life in Mérida, his birth place; it is an aesthetic language filled with deep messages that go beyond the normal sense and intention of traditional reading. His art vision has been a deep component of his work both inside and outside of his studio, which have been presented in collective expos of photography, object-art, and fine art. However, most of his work is less publicly involved, created in private and in an intensely personal manner, working consciously and creatively inside his studio.

A child is at the living room table drawing on a blank sheet of paper with an array of colored crayons that will shame a rainbow. Every other detail around the child fades away and child and crayons sit alone without distractions as the little artist perceives only the paper, the crayons and the drawing that is being created.

The child maintains such great focus, face so close to the paper, it's almost as if the child is trying to enter the paper. Strokes of colors overcome the paper and generate various shapes; some can be recognized, some cannot. The child uses all the colors in the box of crayons, but sometimes one color is used more than others (blue, it seems, is the color most in demand).

Time is passing and the only way to tell if the clock is still ticking is to lay around the child all the colorful artwork that has been created. Even as an adult approaches, the child continues to draw without slowing down, crayon furiously blotting out the white of the paper.

The adult speaks:

"What are you doing?"

"Draw pictures."

"What are you drawing?"

"Whatever."

"Are these drawings for someone?"

"No."

"Do you want to sell them?"

"No."

"Do you want to expose them?"

"No."

"Then why do you draw them?"

"Because."

This story epitomizes the foundation of all good design and highlights the studio axiom we firmly pursue: create because you can create, for creation's sake. Creation is not to surpass, nor to pursue remuneration. It is not for prize or money; we believe in the idea of creating "because."

To Bienal, a brand is a concept and an experience, but most importantly, it means that we have to participate in all possible disciplines to make the best project possible. We believe that cooperation is essential, because only through cooperation can we create a truly functional, aesthetic, homogeneous, and metaphysical experience. The core concept of the project is its own DNA.

As a studio, we have access to numerous resources throughout the entire conceptualization and design of the project, such that we can fully understand each new job. This is why we strive to define and *re*-define ourselves. We prefer to think of ourselves as a narrative, art and design studio rather than a brand studio. We think that the word "brand" points to a limited idea—it is a short list of items, including logos, stationery and selected applications. We believe in the importance of the basic concept and we insist that experience, smell, music, and narrative can be integrated to become an important foundation of the brand; this is the most important element when generating the overall design.

Creation is incredible. It opens an extraordinary world to children and helps adults learn. We can only regain our love for creation by feeling the same excitement that the child in the story feels, engrossed in wielding crayons. The power of these emotions is often underestimated and, dismayingly, slowly lost as we strive to become more academically inclined.

In the story, the child engages with only two physical elements: the colored crayons and the blank, white sheets of paper. With these materials, the child creates without expectation, making something without want of anything in return; no coveting of medals, applause, or money, but creating just *because*. Ignoring the notion that a reward of any kind may exist beyond the reward that is, which is the joy of creating, can be liberating to creativity.

Only by freeing ourselves from these detractors, can we get rid of the burdens of perfectionism, inner expectations, and outer influences that risk of taking us away from our origin. These "dangerous" rewards are the implied shackles of an informed adult—a confined being unable to pursue a creative endeavor without a purpose or prize in mind. We believe that creativity occurs just because, as an instinct. Creation is in itself a reward.

The projects featured in this book reference places that serve as havens for our young generations. These wee, unassuming, non-judgmental souls without apparent experience are the best examples to explain true passion to create. To understand the creative projects in these pages, one must become an unlearned adult so that one may recover the impetuous emotions of a child. Only then we can see through a child's eyes and perceive these spaces and concepts as channels to creation.

The spaces where children grow, experience, play, and create must be vehicles of beautiful creative detonations that contain the proper conditions for them to live, learn, and explore their creative capacities. We are honored to participate in this book as ushers of this experience, and also within the pages as a project feature, showcasing an engaging space that we designed.

This book is full of unrestricted geniality and it is a notable compilation of over 35 projects focused on spaces tailored for the use of the most creative beings in the universe: children. They are surrounded by characters, spaces, colors, interventions, architecture, signages, games, landscapes, and applications that inspire and facilitate their ludic development on one common ground: motivating and exploring.

Education

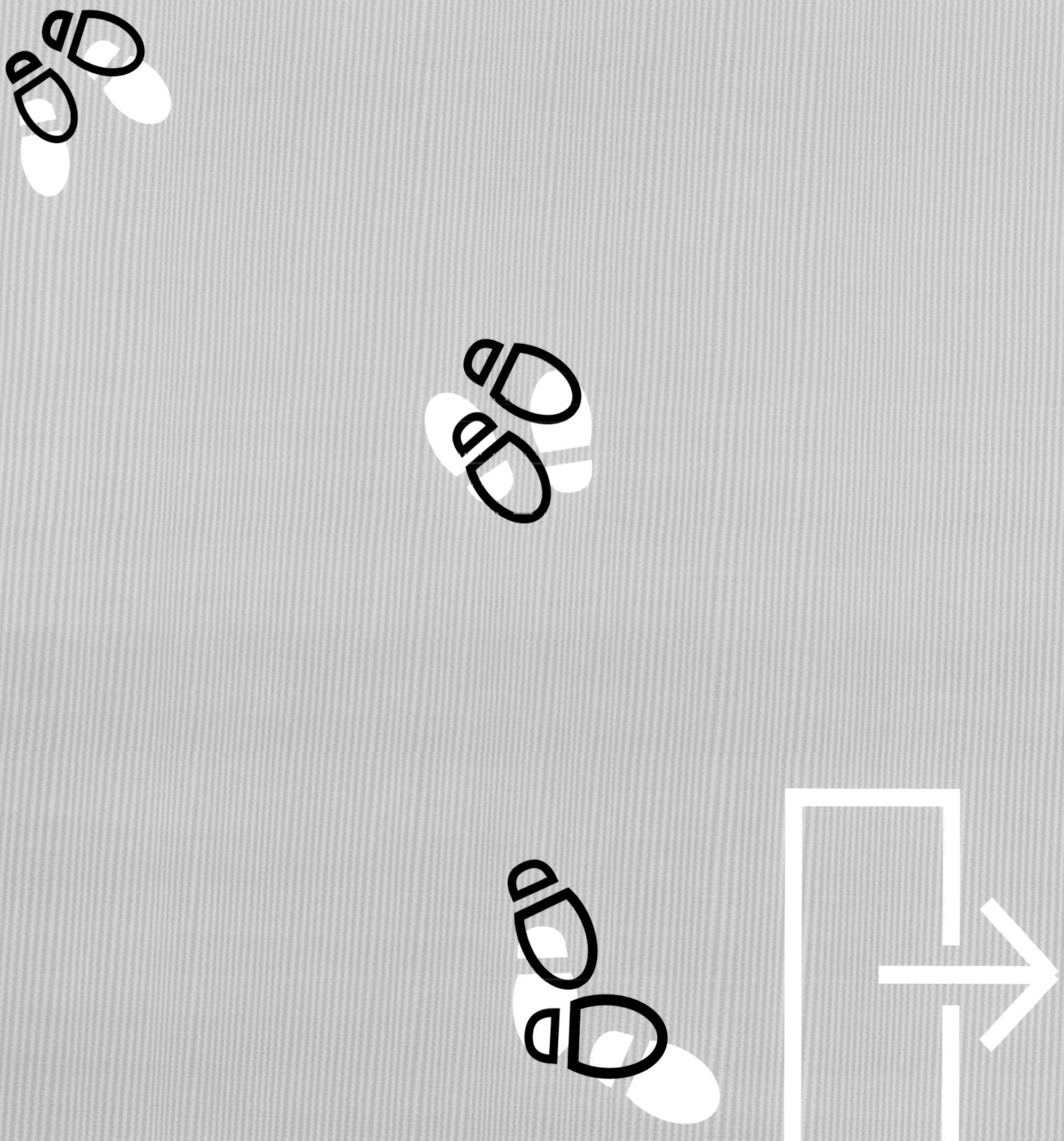

MO Kindergarten

Location: Kyiv, Ukraine

Completion: 2018

Design: about agency

Photography: about agency

This kindergarten based in Kyiv, Ukraine takes on a new name and dynamic brand identity. Its original name, “Kidsworld,” was a mouthful for children and difficult to pronounce, calling for a name change as the first step in the revamp. The new name “MO” has better memory recall and is easier for young children to articulate. On top of that, the letters “M” and “O” can be transformed into funny monster drawings, creating unique characters that add personality to the brand and the physical space. The full name and logo read: “МО. Дитячий садок МОжливостей,” which translates to: “a kindergarten of new opportunities—in innovative education, 24/7 safety, and flexibility for kids and their parents.”

The visual language in children’s spaces such as schools and kindergartens are often boring and unmotivating, and does not engage with them, sometimes resulting in reluctance to go to school. Creating a dynamic brand identity, which translates to a prominent visual identity was, therefore, essential; a relatable “logo-sound” and “logo-emotion” to go along with it was also important. Inspired by cartoons, an animation tone increases engagement and the likelihood of acceptance among children.

Yellow as the main color invokes a bright, sunny mood that depicts fun and play all-year-round. The secondary colors are similarly bright, but sway toward pastel tones to allow for ease of RAL adaptation within the interior. The creative and attractive visual designs and images invite children to create their own fantasies so school becomes more of an adventure, where the world is as big and magnificent as the imagination wills it.

Дитячий садок
можливостей
МОжу все!
Та
ти
шо
я хочу
в

MO Lively
1

Дівчатка

Hello!
Hello!
МАМО,
Я ХОЧУ В
ТОМУ ЩО
ВСЕ
ДЛЯ МЕН

Мамо, хочу в МО!
Та ти шо
Ціноутворення
Карта Weekdays
15 600 грн
Інвестиційний внесок
15 000 грн
Політика лояльності
Для МОго розуму
Для МОго тіла
Для МОго розвитку
MO Kids World
Hello!

Hello!

Noon Afterschool Care

Location: Mérida, Yucatan, Mexico

Completion: 2016

Design: Bienal

Photography: Bienal

Noon Afterschool Care was established as a space for children to develop their minds and skills through fun activities after school hours. In Merida, school hours end between noon and 2 p.m., after which extra-curricular activities are conducted.

The Noon facilities provide a safe and caring environment for children to spend their after-school afternoons; it's an innovative, fun, and attractive space in which they can learn through playful and artistic tasks aimed at developing cognitive, intellectual, and motor skills.

To carve out the brand identity, the inner workings of children's minds and their different styles and ideas were analyzed. The creativity of children is ever-changing, and their awe over the littlest of things is a joy to behold. Inspired by this innocent wonderment, the brand identity looks to the captivating work of Alexander "Sandy" Calder to mould its core.

Well known for his innovative, kinetic mobiles, Calder never lost touch of his playful side; this is apparent in his art, which pays homage to his child-like spirit. It also reflects his belief that movement and fun are as important as colour and shape.

Capturing this belief, a dispersing dandelion design defines Noon's brand identity. Like Calder's mesmerizing mobiles that dance in the wind drifts, the dandelion seeds bob and sail on the wind, carrying children's imaginations with them to discover unexplored fields, faraway skies, and untold stories. As they fly and spread, the dandelions evoke the concept of generating and disseminating knowledge.

As the children, nicknamed "Noonies," interact and play among these colorful worlds, their emotions and thoughts take flight, lifted by the vibrant shades that color the space. In hand with a conducive architectural design and meticulously planned activities, their path of learning, growing, and cultivating mindfulness is paved on a solid foundation, so that they are poised and ready to "fly" with the ambitious dandelion.

noon

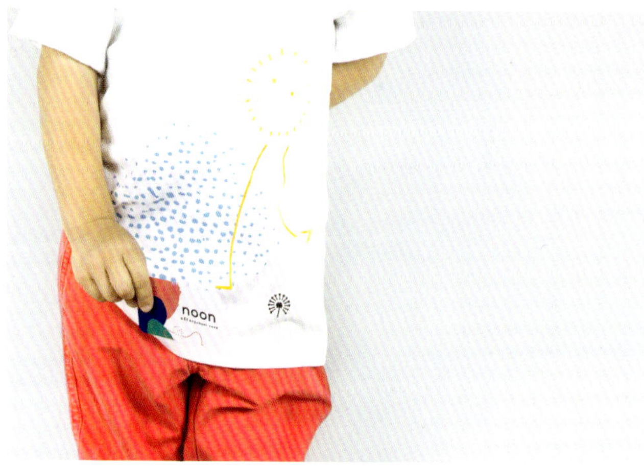
noon

noon
afterschool
care

noon
Bb
noon

noon
afterschool care
noon
afterschool care
noon
afterschool care

villa
noon

Space Dot Kids

Location: Jeju, Republic of Korea

Completion: 2014

Creative Direction: LEE JUNE HYEONG

Art Direction & Illustration: BAE SOO HYUN

Assistant Design: KIM EUN SUN

Photography: KIM YOUNG SOO

Space Dot Kids is a nursery set up by Daum Communications' Jeju island branch, for its employees' children. The visual identity of the nursery reflects the well-loved nature of the island, its prominence in most islanders' day-to-day, and also how it has a hand in nurturing the children on the island.

The wordmark is designed in vividly colorful alphabets that are arranged in a haphazard order to appear as if it's been scribbled by a child. Graphics of children interacting with nature and the elements (wind, clouds, rain, sun, and grass) harmonize with graphics of Jeju's icons, such as Dolharbang, the Volcanic Cone, and Halla Mountain to decorate the interior space with engaging representations of the children's everyday life on Jeju. The visuals are simple and arranged freely to form a pictogram that is straightforward and without formality. Illustrating scenes of activity, the characters paint a lively and compelling visual language as they exemplify the heart of Jeju, which beats in tune with nature—a trait that most children in Jeju identify with.

Signages are made with nature-friendly materials, recycled paper, and green products, such as items contained in minimum packaging, or produced from the white Biroh tree and organic cotton. Children in Jeju, grow and learn with nature as a teacher and governess, and Space Dot Kids is an eco-friendly space that enables that connection with nature.

The wordmark mimics a child's scribble in various vibrant colors that include orange, blue, yellow, green, and purple. Designed to captivate and engage young children, the lively character of the wordmark nudges them to pay attention and consider its letters, colors, and uneven arrangement of the lines; this develops their perception and thinking skills, while exposing them to creativity, to encourage them to explore their own creativity. The striking colors call out to their young eye and helps them anchor the brand identity in their minds. It combines with attractive pictograms and sustainable signage to tailor a visual identity that joins with one heart, Space Dot Kids, the nature in Jeju Island, and of course, the children.

space
dot
kids
다음커뮤니케이션 어린이집
스페이스닷키즈

space
dot
kids

Space dot kids
해오름반
이초록
Space dot kids
뭉게구름반
이다음

Space dot kids

가랑비반

별별 산호마을

둥지방

아름드리방

Yasuragi Nursery School

Location: Kyoto, Japan

Completion: 2018

Design: Marble.co

Photography: Marble.co

Yasuragi Nursery School, operated by Tanabe Central Hospital, is an environment that nurtures children to develop and blossom according to their individual capabilities and talents. The visual identity of the school is translated through logo, flyers, school bus design, signage, and graphical elements, such as window paintings.

The logo is loosely shaped like the letter "Y" to tie in with the name "Yasuragi." It resembles a sprouting seed with the leaves representing family and teachers; these two elements combined produce the sprout, which symbolizes the child. The letters of the logo appear like they are bouncing, creating a cheerful and energetic impression, which implies that the combined effort of family and teachers help children to grow up healthy and happy.

The school's lofty layout and sedate décor decide uncomplicated sign designs that revolve around a clean palette with soft hues. Classroom signs are finished in opaque, white acrylic that feature fruit icons, which include strawberry, orange, and apple. The colorful and simple images are easily recognized and communicate a sense of fun; they are also easy to identify, even for very small children.

やすらぎ保育園

いちじほいくしつ

2さい

たもくてきしつ
たもくてきしつ

0さい
0さい

3さい
3さい

やすらぎ保育園
YASURAGI NURSERY SCHOOL
れんらくちょう

ちょうりしつ

Kindergarten Dornbirn Markt

Location: Dornbirn, Austria

Completion: 2016

Design: Sägenvier DesignKommunikation

Photography: Darko Todorovic

The kindergarten in Dornbirn is an urban showcase. Set between the monastery and the town hall, the two-story building accommodates a total of 92 children; it also houses an underground carpark that is accessible to public.

In conceptualizing the signage for the kindergarten, the words of Loris Malaguzzi, creator of the Reggio Emilia pedagogy, served as inspiration. Malaguzzi said, "A child is made of a hundred; a child has hundred languages, hundred hands, hundred thoughts, and hundred ways to think, play, and speak." To encourage a connection and relatability between the children and the space, their designs and drawings—windows into their "hundred worlds"—are employed as resources in orientation tasks. In an engagement session during the construction phase, the children shared their worlds of splendors, drawing and chatting about their space, their places in it, and their many wonderous fantasies. As they spoke freely without inhibitions, as only children do, they traced crayons and colored markers over paper, creating wonderful plants, animals, people, objects and symbols.

Their figures, drawings and writings take key positions in the signalization system. The public carpark is a showpiece that displays the children's illustrations on the pillars and walls, turning the usually gray space into a huge picture book full of marvellous, colorful scenes. (It's probably the friendliest garage in Vorarlberg!)

The living and learning rooms on the upper floor also exhibit drawings and texts by the children. The four group-rooms are designed in different colors, which extend to the furniture as well, to coincide with the children's group colors. This helps get them organized quicker and without confusion during

group sessions as each group can easily make its way to its respective activity room in the matching color.

Conceptual labels and signage labels on concrete walls, glass partition walls, and tarnished surfaces are realized with lettering penned by the children themselves. Children write their words as they hear them, sometimes with twisted letters. This quirk is retained, rather than amended to appease the rules of design, as this lettering in the children's hand adds a touch of whimsical charm to the building.

Visual identity components extend to the kindergarten's as well. Each child is assigned an animal form or symbol unique to that child; no two children have identical animal forms or symbols. These tags provide identification and orientation, and helps the children recognize each other through association with the graphics. The animal forms and symbols are used in the cloakroom, on drinking cups, craft boxes, gym bags, and the children's shelf space.

BÜROS
BESPRECHUNGSRAUM
WC

AUFGANG

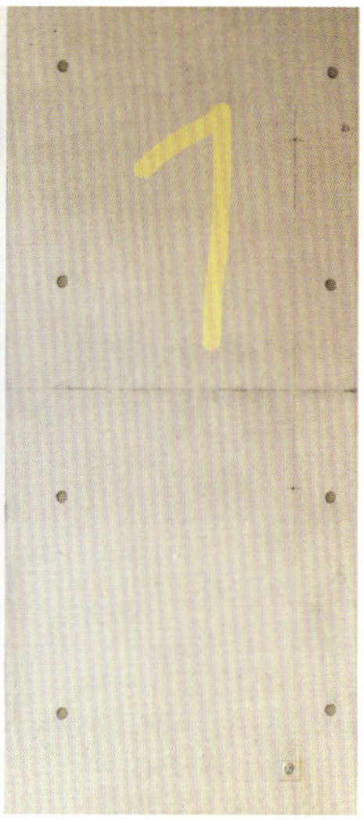

GRUPPEN

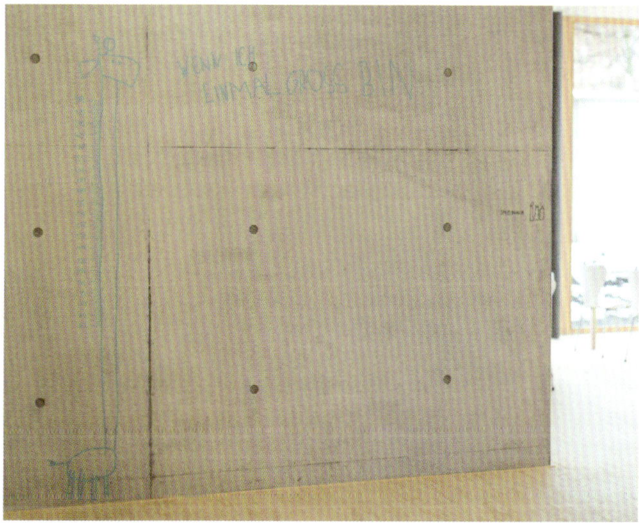

GRUPPEN
LIFT
SPEISERAUM
BEWEGUNGSRAUM
WC

AUS
FAH
RT

DENKA
BESPRECHUNGSRAUM 1

ART4KiDS

Location: Kiev, Ukraine

Completion: 2017

Design: Igor Kolomiiets (Gra Agency)

Photography: Stanislav Cartashov and Alexandra Paskal

ART4KiDS is an art school for children based in Kiev, Ukraine, where students learn to draw and paints with pastels, oils, and other materials. They are also schooled in art history and taught different skills at dedicated workshops, and even go on virtual tours of galleries around the world.

The core of the visual identity presents colored backgrounds made up of scribbles and paint splashes. These elements can be put together in a variety of selections, so that every medium and material is branded with an exclusive background.

To begin, about 400 scribble designs are hand-drawn and uploaded into the background randomizer. It then randomly selects a design, colors, spins, and scales it, and places it against a background; this enables the client to create different designs for different school collaterals, as and when needed, at the simple press of a button. It also ensures that every pattern is unique and there are no two identical designs.

The wordmark defines the brand identity by emphasizing the brand's focus on creativity. The letter's that spell "ART4KiDS" are arranged out of alignment, with the position of each letter altered, to create a dis-organized, artistic look. The letters "i" and "d" also cleverly make a friendly, smiley face that stands out and catches the eye, while expressing a playful, easy-going nature. This new visual identity was launched in 2017, and just over a year after, the school expanded and introduced five new art courses. The best part: no scribble background has been used twice yet.

New Monet
Timur, 12 years
facebook.com/art4kidskyiv
instagram.com/art4kids_kyiv
Провулок Алли Горської, 5
+38 067 469 4985
BigBoard
044 585-99-88

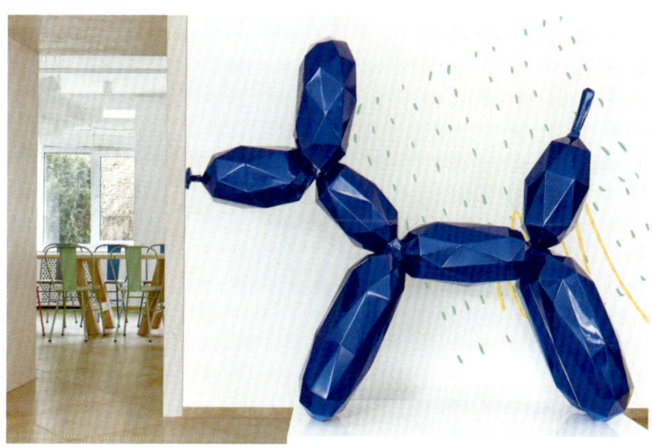

Дитяча художня студія
від 6 до 13 років
ART4 KIDS
facebook.com/art4kidskyiv
instagram.com/art4kids_kyiv
Провулок Алли Горської, 5
+38 067 469 4985
Студія ART4KIDS запрошує на заняття з творчості по буднях та воркшопи й лекції з мистецтва по суботах!
Для усіх охочих від 6 до 13-ти років
Детальніше тут:
instagram.com/art4kids_kyiv
facebook.com/art4kidskyiv
+38 067 469 4985
20.01 Пабло Пікассо
27.01 Анрі Руссо

Арт-студії Art4Kids
Цей диплом засвідчує, що
успішно прослухала(в) курс лекцій
«Мистецтво з пелюшок» і тепер з першого погляду
відрізнить Анрі Руссо від Марка Шагала.
facebook.com/art4kidskyiv
instagram.com/art4kids_kyiv
Провулок Алли Горської, 5
+38 067 469 4985

Подарунок для тебе!
Заняття в студії Art4Kids
Імпресіонізм та ще 10 «...ізмів» в історії мистецтва
1
бал

Імпресіонізм та ще 10 «...ізмів» в історії мистецтва
Мистецтво з пелюшок
ART4 KIDS
Menu
mini cafe
Espresso-20
Lungo-25

ART4 KIDS
ART4 KIDS
10
З цим абонементом можна відвідати 10 занять в дитячій студії мистецтв Art4Kids. Термін дії — один місяць з дати продажу.
facebook.com/art4kidsyiv
Провулок Алли Горської, 5
+38 067 469 4985

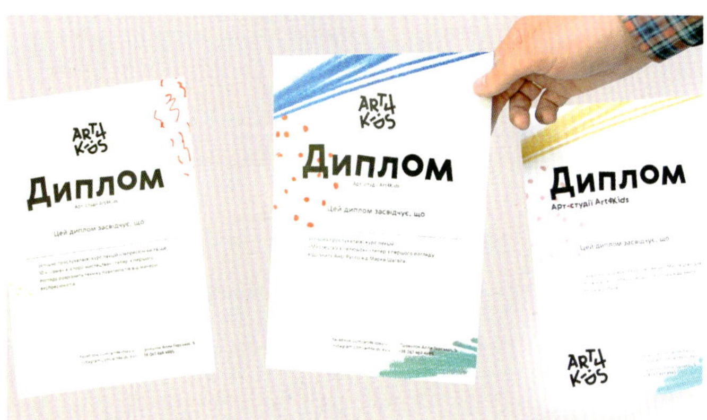
ART4 KIDS
Диплом
Цей диплом засвідчує, що
ART4 KIDS
Диплом
Цей диплом засвідчує, що
Диплом
Арт-студії Art4Kids
Цей диплом засвідчує, що
ART4 KIDS

Cool Kids Development

Location: Mexico City, Mexico

Completion: 2015

Design: Sentido Arquitectura

Photography: Sentido Arquitectura

Cool Kids Development is a school for children aged six months to 10 years old, and it is focused on educating children through games that challenge their creativity, reasoning, and language skills. This 1, 690-square-foot (157-square-meter) facility is located inside a shopping mall in Mexico City.

The owners' enthusiasm about new and innovative teaching methodologies presented a great opportunity (and challenge) to design a space that boosts the creativity of its young users. Moving away from traditional graphic language with figurative elements, the design explores and experiments with abstract forms that come together in different stories and narratives. As the child perceives through the seeing glass of imagination, the blue dots on the walls can turn into birds, maybe raindrops, or even bubbles, and the curved lines may become billowy waves, or a bridge across a river, or perhaps, even a piece of fabric waving in the wind.

The open-plan layout comprises three classrooms, open areas for activities, a staff office, medical office, nutritionist and psychologist office, a waiting area, and restrooms. These spaces are distributed within two floors that are connected with a 16-foot-high (five-meter-high) void in the middle.

Cool Kids Development questions the traditional definition of a classroom, designing classrooms as tiny houses to create inspiring and pleasant learning experiences. Carpet flooring allows the children to walk about barefoot in class, putting them in a relaxed and comfortable mode. The tiny houses are built with metal frameworks, wood panel walls, and transparent, acrylic ceiling so that the children can look up at the interesting fabrics hanging from the outer ceiling, which invite imaginations and daydreams to sway and dance along with them.

OOL
DS
elopment

PB
COOL
K DS
Development

Heloísa Negri Pedagogic Ballet School

Location: Maringa, Brazil

Completion: 2019

Design: Ricardo Sanches de Oliveira (DZ9 DESIGN)

Photography: Ricardo Sanches and Maíra Oliveira

Heloísa Negri Pedagogic Ballet School is a pioneer in pedagogical teaching methods for ballet. The brand is repositioned by uniting the classic and the modern to present the school within a delicate, striking and authentic identity. The visual icon represents the letter "H," the first initial of the school's name, and is inspired by the ballet movement Arabesque, imparting the lightness and beauty of this technique by interpreting its posture and curves.

The new color palette embodies the same characteristics. A range of thoughtfully selected tones complement and complete the visual language to help mould a bold and structured brand identity. They also make their appearance in uniforms, with a different color used for each class division (comprising children, adults and professionals), to project a cohesive visual identity. Every detail is tailored to convey the grace of ballet and to gain association in people's minds as a minimalist brand. Through the simplicity of its visual elements, the ballet school strikes a lasting impression and becomes memorable, like a truly great performance.

heloisa negri
ballet pedagógico

heloisa
negri
ballet pedagógico
BALLET
CLÁSSICO
PEDAGÓGICO

heloisa negri
ballet pedagogico

heloisa
negri
ballet pedagógico

hn
ballet
pedagógico
44 3305 4918
Av. das torres, 4782
Jd. Monte rei - Sala 02
Maringá, PR
www.heloisanegri.com.br

heloisa negri

hn

hn

heloisa negri
ballet pedagógico
CRONOGRAMA
hn
ballet pedagógico
heloisa negri
ballet pedagógico
44 3305 4918
Av. das torres, 4782
Jd. Monte rei - Sala 02
Maringá, PR
www.heloisanegri.com.br

hn

hn
ballet
pedagógico

NUBEL

Location: Shenzhen, China

Completion: 2015

Design: 1983ASIA and Lu Shenyi Creative Studio

Photography: 1983ASIA

NUBEL is a learning platform which aims to help parents and children grow together through experiential teaching philosophies tailored to stimulate children's interest. It believes that "no hug should be forgotten, [as] every hug shines with an extraordinary secret."

The hugging koalas mascots in the logo contribute to a prominent strong visual identity that is appealing to children and easy to recall and recognize, even by young children. This image is not only used in the interior space, but also on brand products, such as stationery, tableware, and uniforms. The dominating color scheme is bright yellow, creating a lively and warm atmosphere. Different logo iterations applied to the many extensions of the brand repeatedly highlight the core value of "parent-child" and gel the brand's visual identity. Beyond that, it also establishes connection, conveying comfort and happiness as children imagine the warm, safe embrace of their parents.

nubel
諾貝抱抱

nubei

游戏区
办公区
OFFICE AREA
美术区
ART AREA
音乐区
MUSIC AREA
烹饪区
卫生间
TOILET

nubel
nubel

nubel

nubel
諾貝抱抱

nubel
nubel

nubel

nubel
nubel
nubel
nubel
nubel
nubel

nubel

nubei

nubei
游戏区
办公区
OFFICE AREA
美术区
音乐区
卫生间
TOILET

Sainte-Anne Academy

Location: Dorval, Canada

Completion: 2015

Design: Taktik Design

Photography: Maxime Brouillet

Award: Grands Prix du Design

This new preschool and primary school of the Sainte-Anne family narrates its visual identity through room layout, furniture design and communication elements, such as signage. Qualifying concepts garnered carte blanche to create an efficient environment that can accommodate the latest teaching standards, just as it is built to inspire—such that it is more a blank canvas for creativity and less an interpretation of imaginations.

In keeping with innovative, international teaching methods, spaces are opened up to create clear sightlines and connections between functions. This layout also encourages light to flow freely so that areas are appropriately illuminated to be conducive for learning. Thematic rooms like the "greenhouse" and "theatre" support teachers in their work, as well as the overall education program. For furniture, seven hundred sheets of plywood form pieces that cater to specific needs: cost-effective, yet solid and easy to clean. Beyond aspects of durability and ease of maintenance, the furniture is also designed to strengthen the visual identity conceptualized around the children using the space; storage units in classrooms and coatrooms are made smaller than normal, tailored to the size of children to allow ease of access.

A color chart and special signage affirm the visual language while instilling a sense of belonging within students; it also aids in orientation, especially of younger students. Each grade is assigned a color and it is ensured that the color is clearly visible from the hallways so that children can quickly locate their classrooms. Monochrome schemes in classrooms prevent visual overstimulation, allowing the children themselves to bring the space to life. Icons representing the institution's values are placed on the walls and included on signage, contributing to the unique character of each learning space. The same shapes are used throughout in varying scales to ensure consistency and strengthen the visual identity of the school.

ACADÉMIE - ACADEMY
SAINTE-ANNE
ALIMENTATION
SANTÉ

DIRECTION

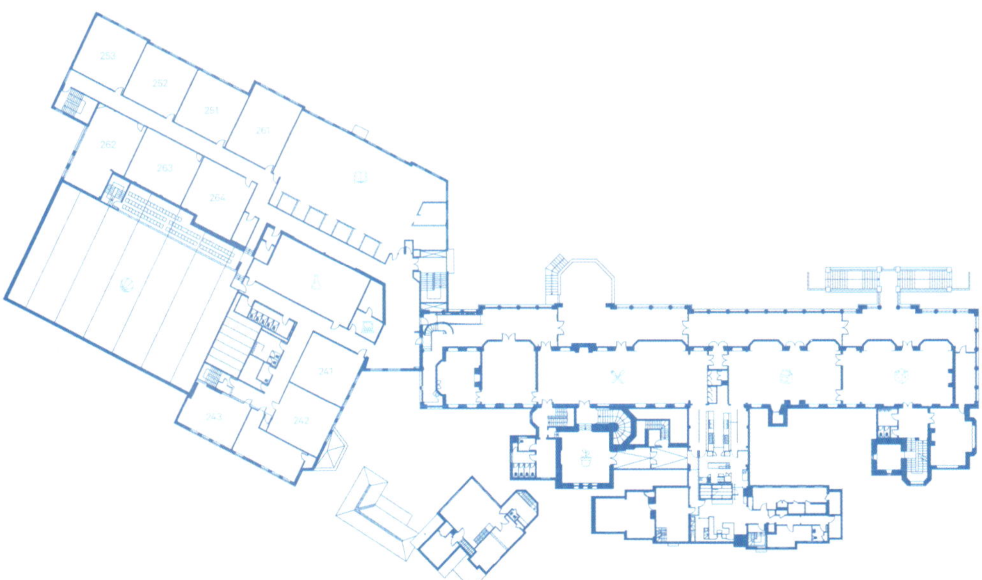

PLOUF
POW
BLOP

THEATRE

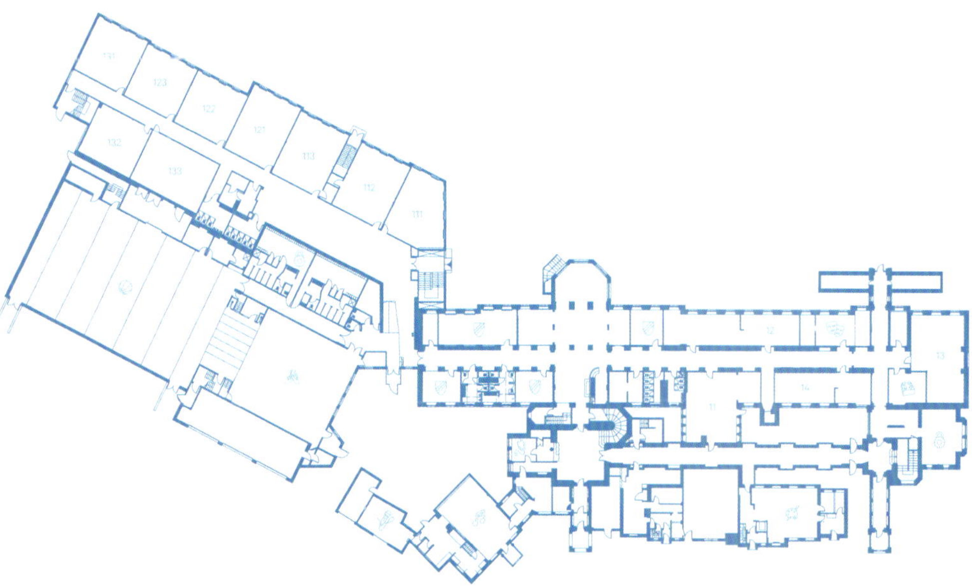

MIAM!
YUM!

112

264

DIRECTION
PRINCIPAL'S OFFICE
SECRÉTARIAT
SERVICES PÉDAGOGIQUES
EDUCATIONAL SERVICES
1ER, 2E ET 3E CYCLES
1ST, 2ND AND 3RD CYCLE
GYMNASE
GYMNASIUM
STUDIO DE DANSE
DANCE STUDIO
BIBLIOTHÈQUE
LIBRARY

Tiny Humans

Location: Mérida, México

Completion: 2017

Design: Puro Diseño

Photography: Paola Boyance

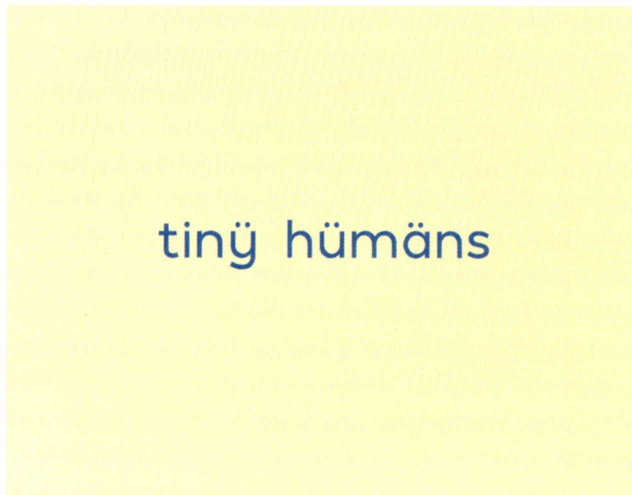

The attributes of current society demand an altered approach in educating and nurturing the minds and characters of young children. Tiny Humans nursery provides a new education vision for the family and school, as necessitated by society today.

"Not simply being a place for learning, but a stage in the lives of children, in which we as adults guide them to create firm foundations illuminated by happiness, since these will define the next stages of the growth of our little ones. Only by educating happy children will we make them capable." With this philosophy as a guide, the slogan of Tiny Humans aptly reads: "#HappyHood."

Together with an architecture and interior design partner, an integral space which communicates a visual identity to match the brand philosophy is created. Colors and visual images that make up the graphical elements of the visual identity decorate classrooms, the façade, and even event materials to enforce visual cohesion.

The visuals allude to the vague, obscure strokes that children draw in their early years and includes a hand design as children easily identify with such natural and straightforward visual outfits. It also allows them to be a part of their own learning process as it presents a familiar form that is simple, easily understood, and easy to relate to.

The simplicity in the brand identity is also observed in the typeface: formal, clean, and direct, with a touch of fun accents. The font type playfully affixes selected letters in the name "Tiny Humans" with eyes to make the wordmark fun and engaging. The pastel color palette is carried through in the interior and induces a soothing ambiance in the space, which fosters the perception of being protected. This helps create an environment in which children feel safe and free to grow and learn. As the ability to learn is not defined by age, the brand image is accordingly defined around the capacity to learn, for each student in Tiny Humans is considered a capable human being from their first months of life.

tinÿ hümäns

tinÿ hümäns
Alexa Garcia
#Happy Hood
T. 9 44 31 17
C. 9999 68 16 11
M. contacto@tinyhumans.mx
www.tinyhumans.mx

tinÿ hümäns

#Happy Hood

tinÿ hümäns
¡Felicidades!
al alumno
Santiago
Por completar el curso 2017-2018 en tiny humans.
1 Septiembre '17
Fecha
Firma

My 1st
tinÿ
hümäns
year

"Children do better when they feel better"

Volksschule Edlach

Location: Dornbirn, Austria

Completion: 2016

Design: Sägenvier DesignKommunikation

Photography: Darko Todorovic

In Volksschule Edlach, the traditional classroom is transformed into a launch site for a variety of teaching techniques built around new pedagogical concepts to drive the school's focus on interdisciplinary learning. Successfully implementing these concepts weigh on an intelligent signaling system, which is achieved through an emblematical flag system: striking ceiling flags provide spatial orientation quickly and without complication; class flags create identity points to gather the "tribes;" colored cluster flags help in locating and coordinating; and special class flags position the children within the school's class-level structure.

The flag system creates a circle of fellowship in the room and even becomes a part of new rituals: class flags can be ceremoniously handed to supporters or used to mark an identity and forge class spirit in school events. In keeping with the ancient tradition of flags, animal insignias establish heraldry to strengthen community and cohesion among students.

The signage typography is modern with a gentle, playful character. Signs are placed on surfaces instead of directly on doors, so that they remain visible instead of concealed, even when doors are opened. In some areas, they are placed behind plexiglass panels, making them appear like they are floating; this way, they can also be easily replaced, if so needed.

In some areas, graphic elements with the same characteristics of the typography make up illustrative narratives around the heraldic animal insignias. On staged glass and tarnished surfaces, these captivating figures romp about and populate the school's living space together with the children, telling of a fabulous world of fun and games.

Aula

↑ Cluster 1+2+3
Vorschulklasse
Garderobe
WC Buben

Cluster 4+5
← Direktion
Idee-Café
Aufzug
→ Ausgang
Aula
Sporthalle
↑ WC barrierefrei

2B
1

3

Sprachförderung

Entertainment & Leisure

Ancymondo Play Zone

Location: Lodz, Poland

Completion: 2019

Design: Politanski Brand Design

Photography: SebasBan Glapinski (Platin Studio)

Ancymondo is a colorful world that has been created for Stacja Nowa Gdynia Business & Wellness Resort on the outskirts of Lodz, Poland. It is a children's play zone that loudly announces play and fun for children (and their accompanying adult) with a creative variety of activity stations set to raise excitement, while weaving in opportunities to learn and explore.

The name "Ancymondo" means a land (in Italian "*mondo*") of rascals (in Polish "*ancymon*"), and it is a unique place full of attractions where small and big "rascals" rule, accompanied by cheeky creatures called Ancystwory ("*stwór*" in Polish translates to creature). The Ancystwory are funny, smiling beings always eager to play, and they take over the walls in crazy shapes and vivid colors.

To develop a comprehensive brand identity, a friendly visual concept that appeals to all age groups is created. These criteria also allow the concept to be used across various media without too much fuss.

The color palette is characteristically striking and eye-catching, allowing ads and marketing materials to stand out in the urban space and draw attention without effort.

Every detail, down to the tiniest implementations, are meticulously thought-out to ensure that promotional materials and marketing complements/toys are attractive and useful to both little and big guests of Ancymondo. Wordmark in a friendly typography help the materials make pleasant impressions, while remaining legible. The visual identity is extended to the website layout and social media channels to maintain cohesion and tailor a strong, holistic brand identity.

Colorful advertising campaigns kickstarted the launch, informing residents in Lodz and nearby areas of Ancymondo as a "new, extraordinary place on the city map." Communications were kept simple and short without giving away too many details, unveiling the mystery just before the grand opening. The design is well-received, as seen in the enthusiasm of the kids who eagerly explore and play in the extraordinary world of Ancymondo.

ancy
figle
Już niebawem
w nowej figlostrefie!
ancymondo
STACJA NOWA GDYNIA
ancymondo.pl
ams

ancymondo
FIGLOSTREFA

← droga
do dobrej
zabawy
ancymondo

→ tam czeka
na Ciebie
figli moc
ancymondo

1215
figli moc!
ancymondo
STACJA NOWA GDYNIA
figli
Wszystkie urwisy
mile widziane!

Hej!
Serwus!
ancymondo

ancymondo
ancy atrakcje!
cennik figli

ancymondo
cennik figli
ancy urodziny!
ancy atrakcje!
figli moc!

figli moc!
ancymondo.pl
ancymondo
STACJA NOWA GDYNIA

Ancyjubilat
Adrian
Ancyjubilat
ancymondo
KARTA CZŁONKOWSKA
bawię się z
Olkiem
bawię się z
ancymondo
KARNET NA ZABAWĘ
ancymondo.pl
ancymondo.pl
ancymondo.pl
ancymondo.pl

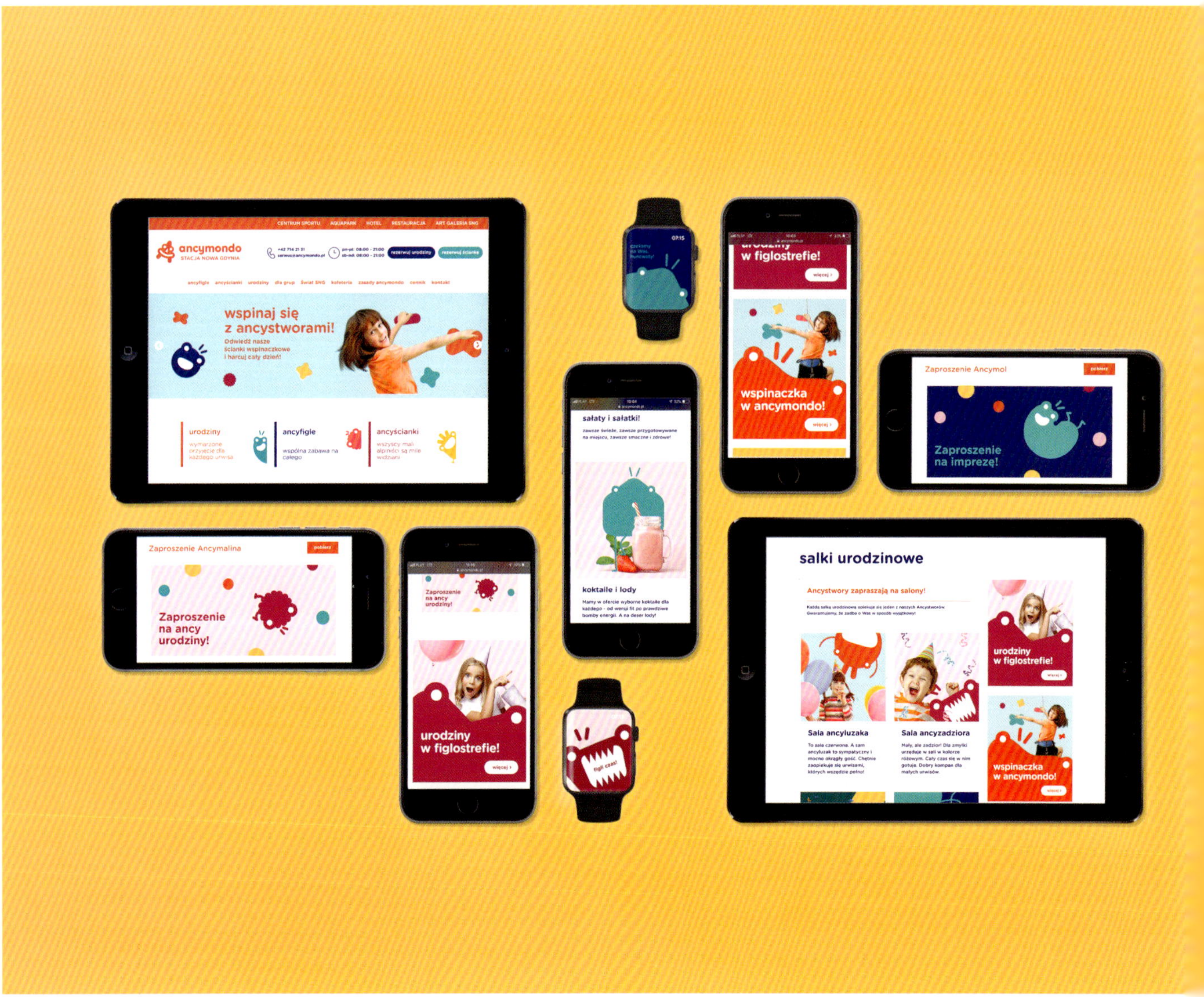
ancymondo
wspinaj się z ancystworami!
urodziny
ancyfigle
ancyścianki
w figlostrefie!
wspinaczka w ancymondo!
sałaty i sałatki!
koktaile i lody
Zaproszenie Ancymol
Zaproszenie na imprezę!
Zaproszenie Ancymalina
Zaproszenie na ancy urodziny!
urodziny w figlostrefie!
salki urodzinowe
Ancystwory zapraszają na salony!
Sala ancyluzaka
Sala ancyzadziora
urodziny w figlostrefie!
wspinaczka w ancymondo!

sto lat,
sto lat!
ancymondo
animator
ancyfigli

ancymondo
FIGLOSTREFA
ancymondo.pl

hip, hip,
hurrraa!

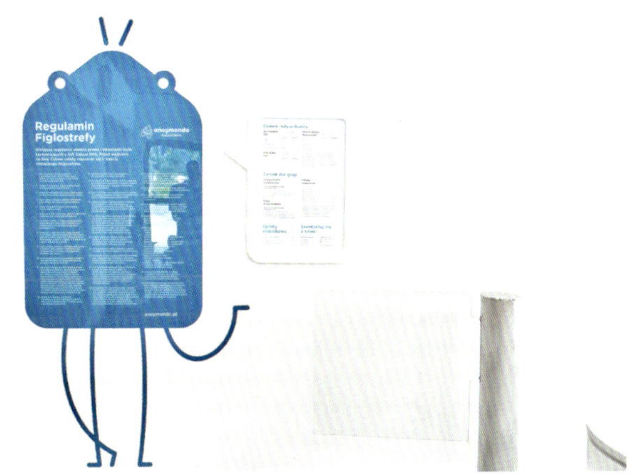
Regulamin
Figlostrefy
ancymondo

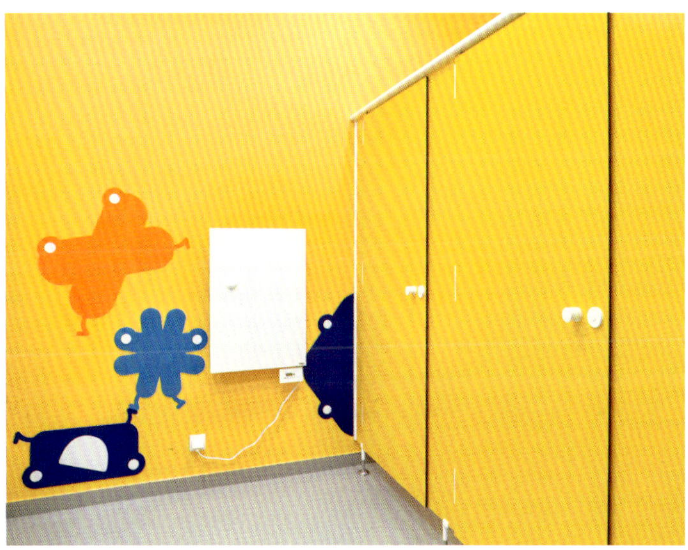

Blue Marine Sports Club

Location: Nagano, Japan

Completion: 2019

Design: Arata Takemoto Design, Toshiaki Mizuma, MON architects

Photography: Tomooki Kengaku

The facility was opened in spring 2019 and features an atrium and an uncomplicated, smooth circulation that seamlessly connects the space. To take advantage of this, the visual identity is narrated through environment graphics, which create zone-specific designs that encourage users to interact with the space.

The entrance hall introduces a unique, playfully tiered staircase against a white wall that is randomly scattered with colorful letters, inspired by the concept of "word bouldering;" as the eye trails from the bottom up, letters of the same color "climb" and connect to form positive words such as "future" and "peace." Design details are set out subtly, rather than conspicuously, such that users who visit regularly will chance upon them randomly, keeping the experience of the space engaging and filled with discovery.

The wall next to the reception takes on an equally playful persona with a painted-on high-jump measure that invites candid leaps from those who pass. As the children test their high jump skills, they are motivated to top their reading with a higher jump the next time round, encouraging a zest for sports and personal strive. Shoe racks and lockers are decorated with animal faces and colors instead of numbers to extend the theme of fun, inviting enthusiastic guesses to identify the animal.

The gallery (viewing space) on the second floor overlooks the swimming pool and offers a visual connection between the two spaces. Children in the gallery can observe the activity by the pool, and the people at the pool can enjoy the distraction of kids' play made special by an approximately 98-foot-long (30-meter-long) wall designed as a backdrop to bring out the children's movements. Other design elements, such as the colorful bars on the floor, may be utilized in a skill-testing game of long jump, or a lively game of leapfrog, any other creative ways to play.

In recent years, the decrease in physical strength and athletic ability of children has become an increasing concern in Japan. The visual elements in the Blue Marlin Sports Club strive to resonate with children and create a positive association with sports in the hope that it will encourage them to exercise more, and also foster strong communication with each other.

260
240
220
200
180
160
140
120
100
80
60
40
20

消火栓

Brella

Location: Los Angeles, California, USA

Completion: 2019

Interior Design&Branding: Project M Plus

Photography: Project M Plus

The goal is to create a space for children that is fun and nurturing, while fostering a sense of community, as well as ensuring it is also aesthetically appealing to parents.

A modern approach specifies sturdy, commercial materials and opts for gender-neutral colors, furniture, art, and accessories. Playful shapes, combined with color schemes that ground light, pastel tones with dark, vibrant hues, provide that the design is not overly infantile. The playful patterns in the Forbo linoleum flooring of the Gross Motors section create a lively zone and is repeated in the restrooms to extend continuity in the design. The furniture, a mix of modern Scandinavian pieces and classic, custom pieces by modern American brands, feature simple, clean lines and soft, rounded edges that are children-friendly.

Color is employed as an integral tool to accentuate the overall experience. The palette is colorful, but refined, without any traditional, primary hues. Combining it with the generous use of wood tailors a space that is soft and welcoming, and warm and relaxing. The magnetic wall in the drop-off area adds a neat design touch that is conveniently also utilitarian.

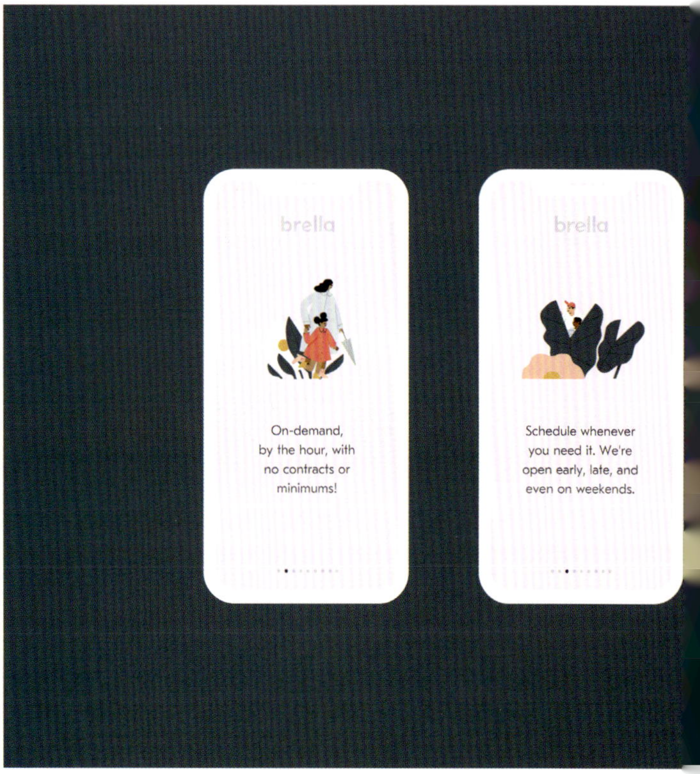

To build connection between the children and the natural world, artist Amelia Giller was commissioned to create a mural. Beautiful, life-size illustrations convey the Brella model of care as being as natural and essential to daily life as the rising sun. The brand and its visual language communicate playfulness, vibrancy, and a community approach to thriving, pairing a hand-drawn artisan layer with clean typography in sans.

This immersive play and workspace universally appeal to boys and girls, and adults and children alike. Design features are singular, grand and broad, with nothing fussy.

brella

ella
e, enriching
ds 3 months
years.

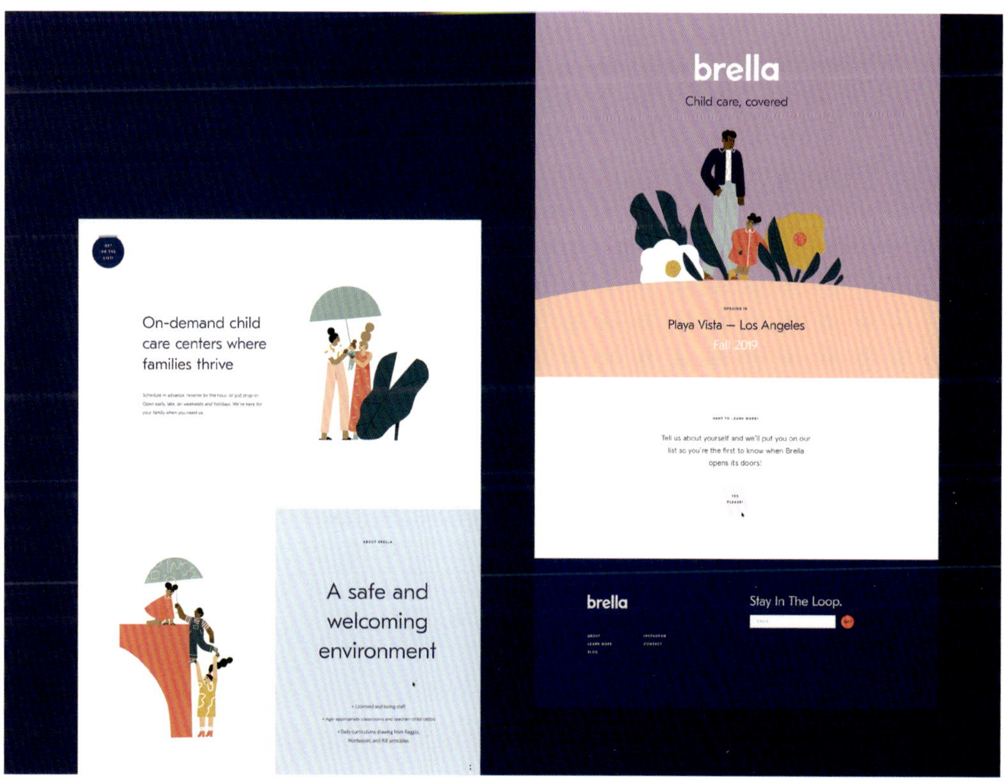
On-demand child care centers where families thrive
A safe and welcoming environment
brella
Child care, covered
Playa Vista — Los Angeles
Fall 2019
Tell us about yourself and we'll put you on our list so you're the first to know when Brella opens its doors!
brella
Stay In The Loop.

brella

EXIT

EXIT

A Visitor for Bear
SO MANY FEET
ABC
Meditate with Me
PEEK and SEEK

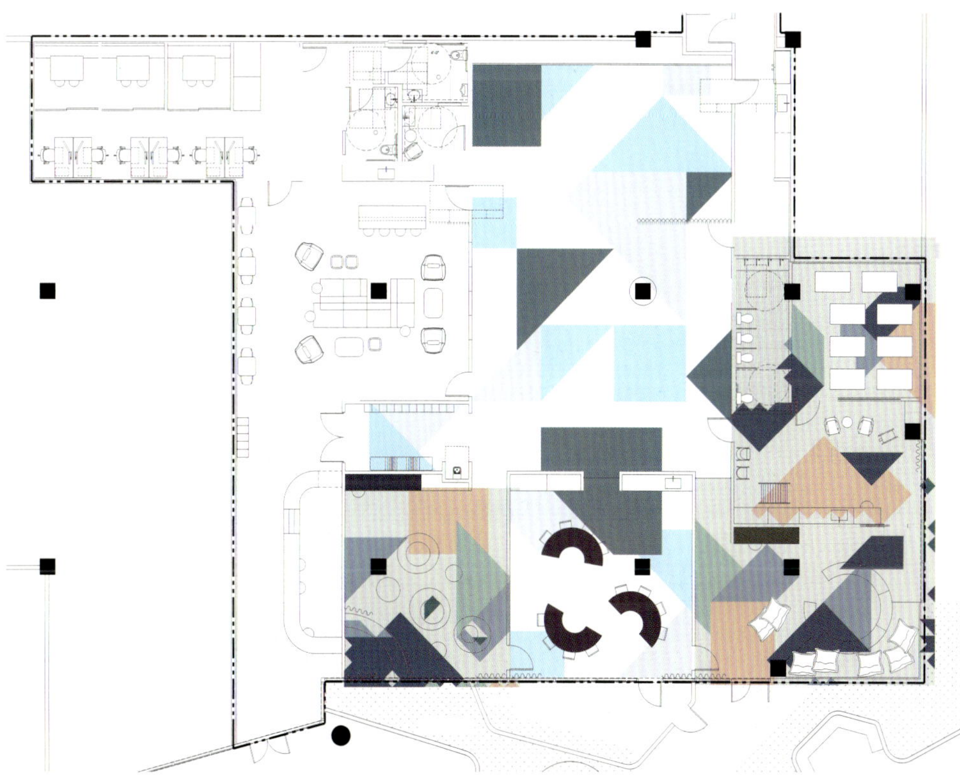

Kidspace

Location: Kazan, Russia

Completion: 2019

Design: Zarina Gayvoronskaya and Vladimir Trinos

Photography: Vladimir Trinos

Kidspace is an experiential, learning, leisure, and enrichment facility where children can learn about various professions through role-play. The brand identity is shaped through the brand name, wordmark style, logo, and colors, and is translated into a comprehensive visual identity by flowing the colors, related imagery, and logo throughout the space in creative variations.

An emblem brand logo features a heraldic coat of arms made of elements that have been specifically selected to embody the spirit of Kisdpace. The flag at the top symbolizes a child's goals, faith and courage and the galaxy/universe revolving around the apple—reflected as Newton's apple, which is a symbol of knowledge—denotes new discoveries that children make at Kidspace, which build their experiences and learning. This coat of arms logo forms the foundation of the visual identity and is splashed across the interior space, as well as used in Kidspace city documents, such as the Kidspace passport. The brand values of friendliness, openness, unlimited imagination and possibilities are also conveyed through engaging illustrations and bright, captivating colors.

Imagery and illustrations not only dress the décor, but they also provide navigation within the city. All décor elements are designed to be part of the game. In Kidspace, the world is created according to the rules of children. Through fun and interactive games, children explore the many professions in the world and learn what they are about in 28 thematic locations. Every child is different with varied interests; each Kidspace location features a unique set of professions, enabling variety that keeps the city and the Kidspace experience engaging. No detail is spared in Kidspace city: money, travel documents, social structure, and laws are just as real as they are in the real world, and through such authentic representations—some chosen by the children themselves—they experience a semblance of the working world and the grown-up life.

Детского города
Удивительного путешествия!

Я ХОЧУХ

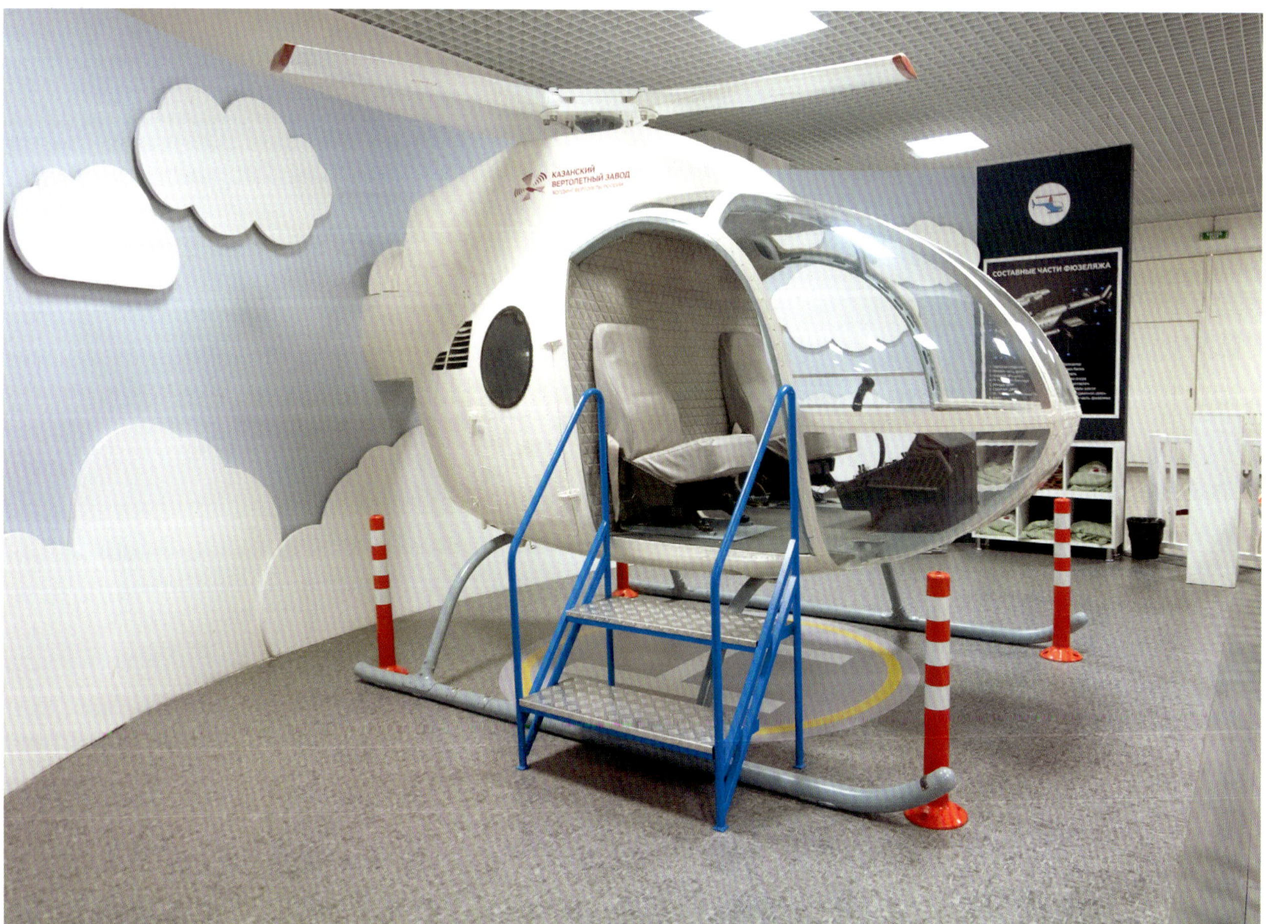
КАЗАНСКИЙ
ВЕРТОЛЕТНЫЙ ЗАВОД
СОСТАВНЫЕ ЧАСТИ ФЮЗЕЛЯЖА

КИДСПЕЙС
ЧЕРЕЗ ОТКРЫТИЯ К ЗВЕЗДАМ
ПАСПОРТ
PASSPORT

С днём рождения! Будь талантливой и оригинальной!
Через открытия к звездам
КИДСПЕЙС
8 ДЕКАБРЯ ОТКРЫТИЕ ПЕРВОГО В КАЗАНИ ДЕТСКОГО ГОРОДА ПРОФЕССИЙ
С днём рождения! Будь смелым и сильным!

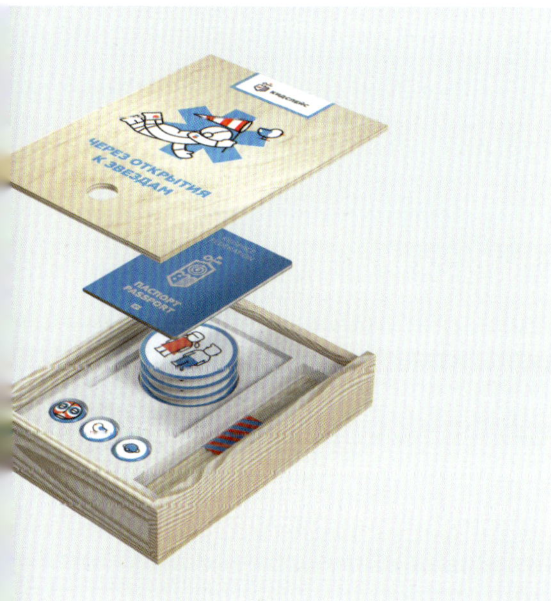
КИДСПЕЙС
ЧЕРЕЗ ОТКРЫТИЯ К ЗВЕЗДАМ
ПАСПОРТ
PASSPORT

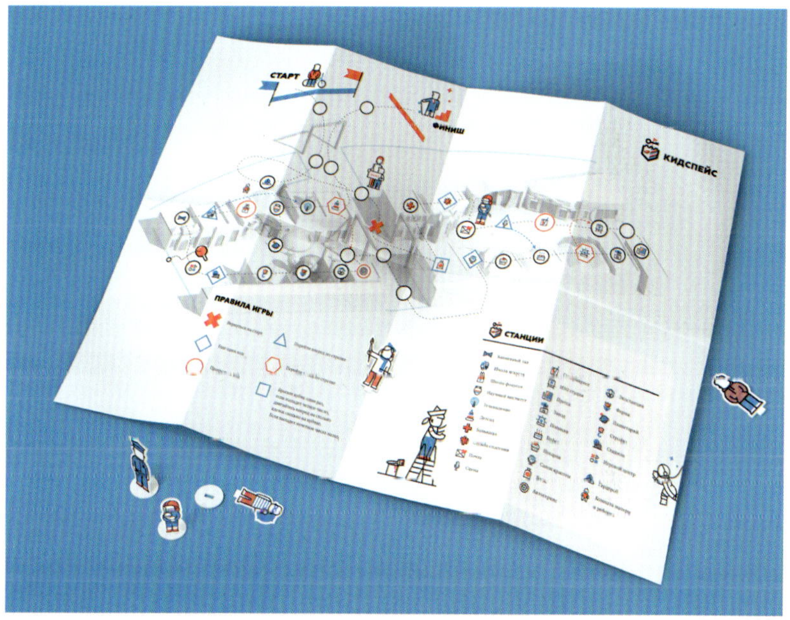
СТАРТ
ФИНИШ
КИДСПЕЙС
ПРАВИЛА ИГРЫ
СТАНЦИИ

ШРИФТЫ
У КАЖДОГО ДЕЛА ЗАПАХ ОСОБЫЙ:
Жил-был принц. Королевство у него было совсем маленькое.

КИДСПЕЙС
KIDSPACE
Уважаемый Иван Иванович!
KID SPA CE
НАТАЛЬЯ

KIDSPACE

БУФЕТ

ГОСТЕВАЯ

MILK KIDS

Location: Tianjin, China

Completion: 2019

Design: New & Mind Studio

Photography: MILK KIDS

Founded in Tianjin, China in 2015 along the brand value of "keeping naivety," MILK KIDS, a parent and children photography studio underwent a brand revamp (three years later) to portray the brand as playful, joyful and true.

The interior space is designed to create a more light-hearted, enjoyable, and intimate atmosphere for parent-child photography, focusing more on the children, than on the background and décor of the space. Just like "MILK," which is white and pure, and a natural nutrition for children, the space aesthetics are simple and natural so as not to deflect attention from the photo subjects. The brand colors of yellow and white are cleverly adapted to the physical space of MILK KIDS defining a playful, yet cozy ambiance that puts children at ease. An informal play and refreshments area ensures that children feel relaxed the moment they enter. It also provides an opportunity to meet the photographer in a welcoming, relatable setting, so that more natural photos can be achieved during the shoot.

The logo is cartoon-like and friendly, represented as mascots that are "older" milk carton and a "younger" milk bottle to be synonymous with the brand's parent-child affiliation. The logo also captures the business of the brand with faces that appear like they are looking through a camera's viewfinder, ready to snap a shot; adding to that are hands that extend to appear as if they are focusing a camera lens. Memorable and eye-catching, the logo is not only appealing to children, but it also embodies what the brand is about. Dressed in the same yellow and white color palette, it leads the visual identity of the brand and marks related brand merchandise, posters, and marketing collaterals in different variations that are just as recognizable.

MILK
KIDS

MILK KIDS
MILK KIDS

MILK KIDS × MILK
MILK family
MILK KIDS
A BAO
阿宝
MANAGER
STAY REAL
MILK KIDS
THE MOST POPULAR CHILD PHOTOGRAPHY IN THE UNIVERSE

MILK KIDS × MILK
MILK family
MILK KIDS · KIDS PHOTOGRAPHY
MILK KIDS
儿童摄影

MILK KIDS × MILK
MILK family
MILK KIDS
MILK KIDS · KIDS PHOTOGRAPHY
MILK KIDS
THE MOST POPULAR CHILD PHOTOGRAPHY IN THE UNIVERSE

MILK KIDS × MILK
MILK family
MILK KIDS
MILK KIDS
STAY REAL

MILK KIDS
儿 童 摄 影
STAY REAL
MILK KIDS 旗艦店
NEW STORE
欢迎
光临
TO THE LEFT 往左
STAY REAL
STAY REAL
MILK KIDS
儿 童 摄 影
全宇宙-
最用心的
儿童摄影
The most popular child photography in the universe
由此进入
COME ON!!
STAY REAL
留住纯真
New Store Opening
MILK KIDS
儿 童 摄 影
NEW STORE OPENING
全宇宙-
最用心的
儿童摄影
The most popular child photography in the universe
STAY REAL
前方进入
COME ON!!
Welcome the MILK KIDS Planet~!

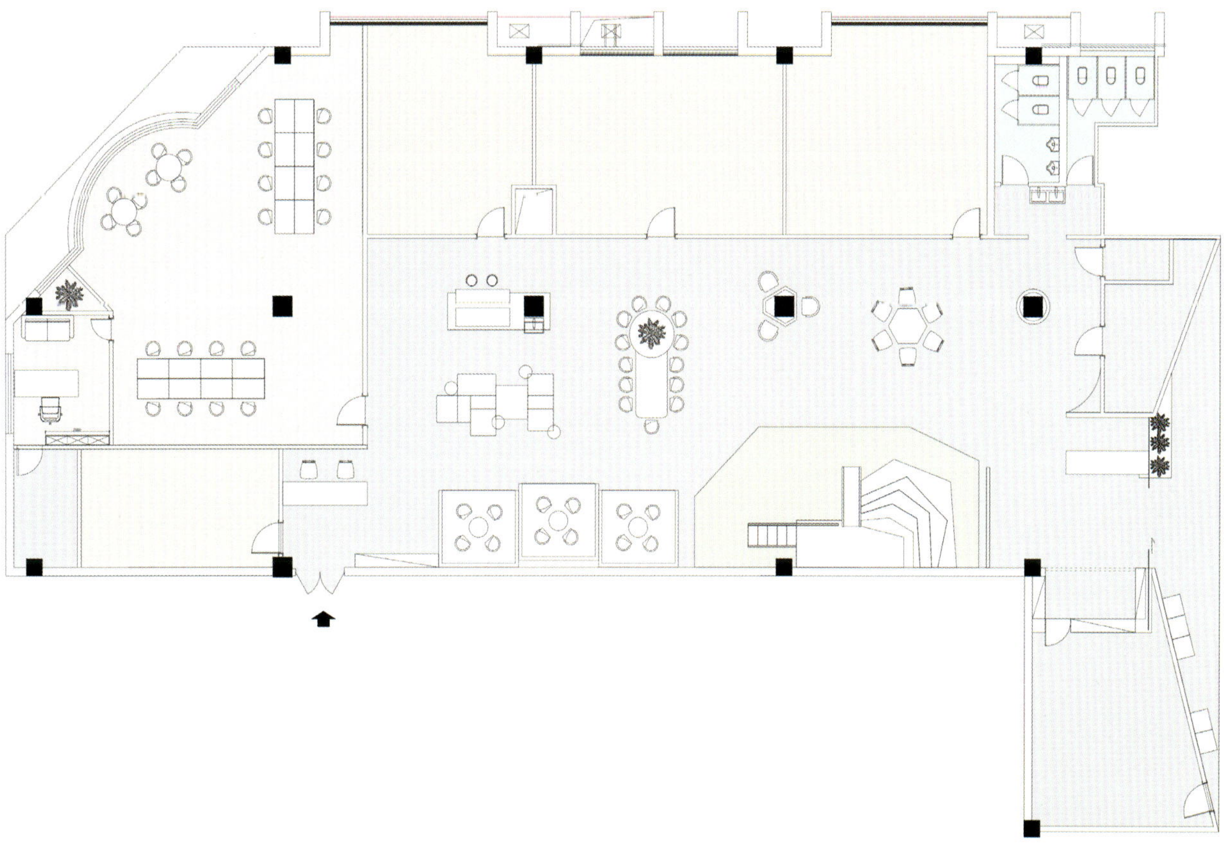

保洁间

ON AIR

MILK KIDS
MILK KIDS
易碎!
勿扔!
The best wish
for you
OPEN~
THE MOST POPULAR CHILD PHOTOGRAPHY IN THE UNIVERSE

MILK KIDS
MILK KIDS
The best wish
for you
OPEN~
STAY REAL
THE MOST POPULAR CHILD PHOTOGRAPHY IN THE UNIVERSE

MILK KIDS
MILK family
MILK KIDS
MILK KIDS
THE MOST POPULAR CHILD PHOTOGRAPHY IN THE UNIVERSE

MILK KIDS
MILK family
MILK KIDS
MILK KIDS
THE MOST POPULAR CHILD PHOTOGRAPHY IN THE UNIVERSE

Thank You
Thanks for your trust.
MILK KIDS

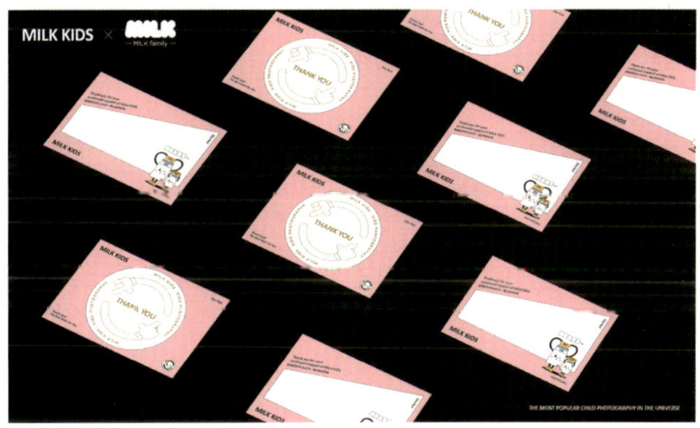
MILK KIDS
MILK family
THANK YOU
THE MOST POPULAR CHILD PHOTOGRAPHY IN THE UNIVERSE

Health

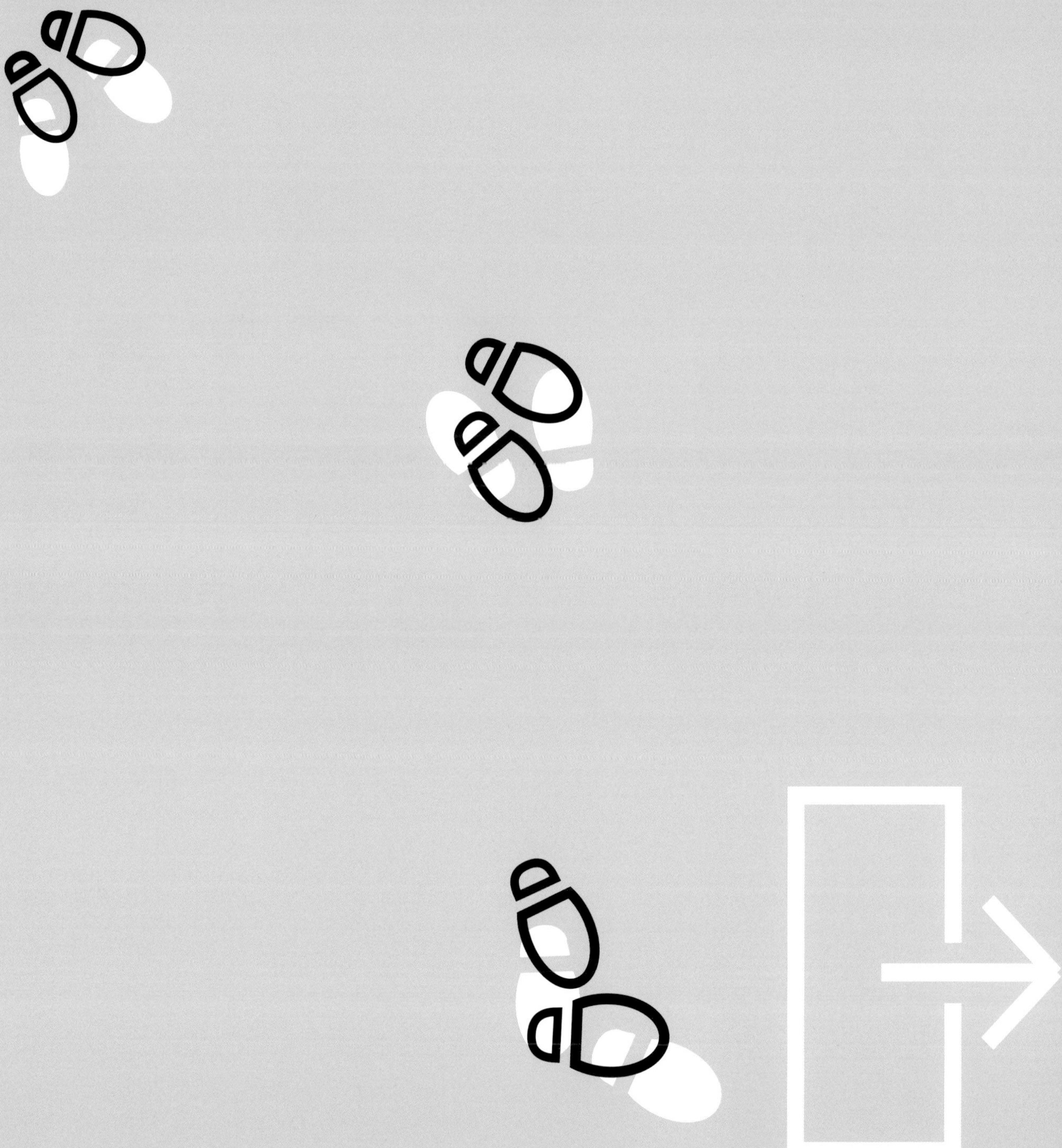

Animals Playing Hide-and-Seek

Location: Barcelona, Spain

Completion: 2013

Design: Arauna Studio and Rai Pinto Studio

Photography: Victòria Gil, Borja Ballbé, Dani Rubio Arauna and Rai Pinto

This project focused on tailoring a friendlier, less ominous ambiance in the recently renovated emergency ward of Sant Joan de Déu Children Hospital in Barcelona. Hospital officials termed this revamp "pediatrization," which is to adapt the space to increase the children's comfort and foster interaction and play in a typically sombre space, such as a hospital.

The concept of animals playing hide-and-seek spins an interesting storyline that is adapted across different areas in the hospital. The visuals are based on real-scale animal shapes that hide behind the hospital's architecture. The animals are portrayed in a repetition of patterns in a fixed color palette and realised as a constant dialogue between two-dimensional and three-dimensional visual outfits. This allows a multitude of interrelated interventions and generates over a hundred different animal visuals scattered across the hospital.

This concept attaches a coherent and cohesive visual identity in a wide space that is over 5,382 square feet (5,000 square meters) in size, while adapting to pre-existing architectural elements. More importantly, it also effectively "pediatrizes" the space as tasked to.

Although this concept was initially conceived as a solution for the emergency ward, it extends across the entire hospital and its outer environment. The signage system in both inner and outer spaces is redesigned to match, so as to maintain a comprehensive and cohesive visual identity that is warm and friendly throughout.

MIAU MIAU MIAU MIAU MIAU

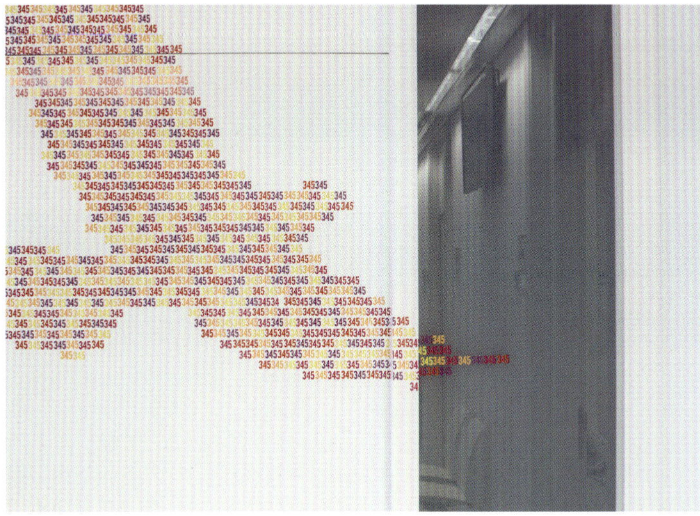

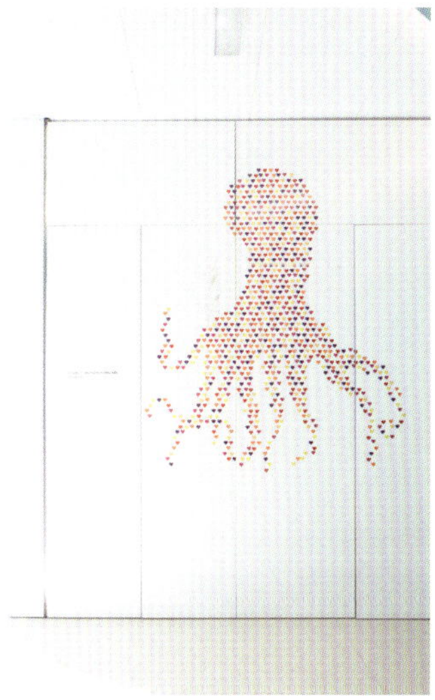

Planta
C3
Cures Pal·liatives
Cardiologia
Genètica
Immunoal·lèrgia
Nefrologia
Neurocirurgia
Oftalmologia
Otorinolaringologia
Pneumologia

308

Grand Jardin de Sainte-Justine

Location: Montreal, Canada

Completion: 2017

Design: Sid Lee

Photography: Cindy Boyce

When Sainte-Justine Hospital, Canada's largest mother-and-child center underwent an expansion, the new, freshly painted walls presented blank canvases that elicited two simple wishes: to portray the hospital's history, and to breathe life into the halls of the new pavilion. Over 5,200 square feet (483 square meters), seven dazzling murals manifest moments in the hospital's past to acquaint them with the present.

Grand Jardin de Sainte-Justine (the Grand Garden) is a magical place filled with mysterious creatures and lively colors that portray more than 100 years of the hospital's rich history through beautiful metaphors. Arranged across a timeline with accompanying descriptions, the murals gain favor with different visitors on different attributes. Teenagers and adults enjoy the artfully delivered history lesson that reveals the hospital's rich past, while children are drawn to the vivid colors and familiar shapes of the design that transport them into their own imaginary worlds. The overlying themes of nature, life and growth convey messages of hope, and dress the walls with flowy, calming illustrations that promote a soothing ambiance.

The materials selected for this project are long-lasting, easy to clean, and easy to install. The design language is inspiring, lively, and universal, compliments of the oversized visuals executed by the concept. The distinct identity of the Garden's visual images even earned them a coloring book of the images, which was distributed during the launch. The gargantuan proportions are key to the impact of the visual elements, for they dutifully build a "larger than life" environment where children and adults eagerly lose themselves.

Répertoire général

le Grand jardin
Répertoire général
la Petite pousse

la Petite pousse
INTRODUCTION
Lacoste-Beaubien et Irma LeVasseur
une lueur d'espoir dans l'univers
Sainte-Justine prend vie.
rencontre, un petit lit est déjà prêt
premier patient. C'est le début d'une
qui se déploiera et changera
d'enfants pour des années à venir.
pousse lancée au vent.

Pour
l'amour
des mères
et des
enfants

la Grande
épopée

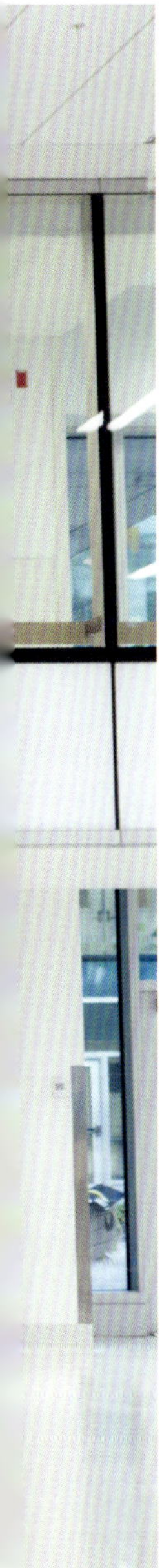

la Grande
épopée

Parc d'Atencions

Location: Barcelona, Spain

Completion: 2015

Design: Toormix

Photography: Adrià Goula

This new day-care hospital sought to be an environment that encourages low stress levels, so as to encourage staff enthusiasm and effort toward delivering quality service. While developing a theme name for the interior space, brand design, visual code, and service design, enabling a convenient and satisfactory user experience was also considered in order to cater an overall holistic user experience in the final outcome. The redesigns focus on three audience groups: the patients, their relatives, and the medical team, with the aim to build a comfortable and friendly environment for all.

The personalities, needs, and perceptions of each patient group is different and the design addresses these different aspects by closely and carefully considering the main differences between each of these groups, made up of babies, children, and teens.

Conceptualized like an amusement park, the new space is aptly named Attentions Park (or Parc d'Atencions), sampling a play of words in its name. Specifically designed as a friendly environment where young people will enjoy and appreciate the care they receive, the new Attentions Park is arranged into three sections: the natural environment, which is the waiting room; the universe, which is the medical consultation area and offices; and the racing circuit, which is the treatment bay. Consideration and concern rank high as young patients and their families are tended to in the areas of medical, personal and emotional care.

Treated organic materials, a three-color palette (green, yellow and orange), indirect and natural lighting, and visuals in three different themes shape the spaces, as well as mark the circulation and distribution of the plan. Calm colors are considerately selected so the the visual implements are not jarring or saturating. This also avoids the error of appealing only to one audience group; many different types of audience coexist in this space, and it is essential that all of them feel comfortable in that same space.

In the area of service design, different spaces are conceptualized and designed in accordance with complicities: tables/co-work zones for family members, play areas/huts with the scale adapted to younger patients, and independence zones for teen patients. The result is a warm, compassionate and considerate treatment environment that is understanding of patients' delicate situations.

ARC
ATENCIONS
nens, nenes i familiars
FJRA
Fundació Joan Ribas Araquistain
Obra Social "la Caixa"
Fundació Vila Casas
ecció mèdica
sep Sánchez de Toledo
Aquest Hospital de Dia és una realitat per l'incondicional suport de moltes
persones que van creure que els somnis impossibles no existeixen.

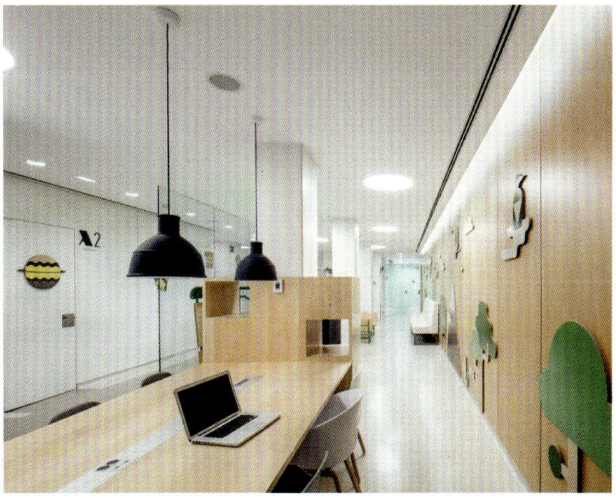

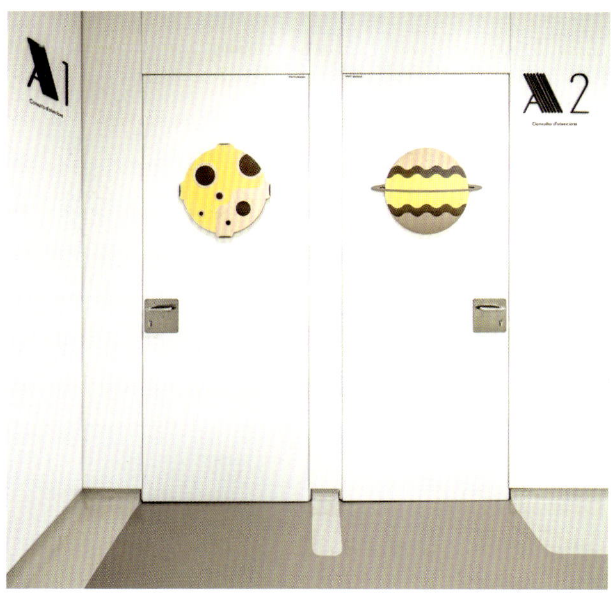

A2
A3

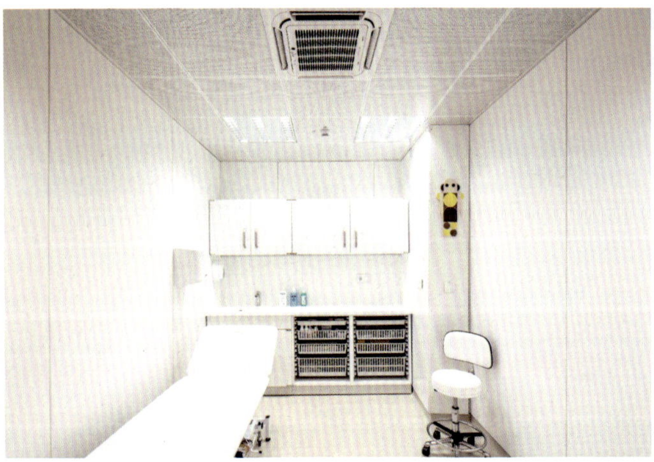

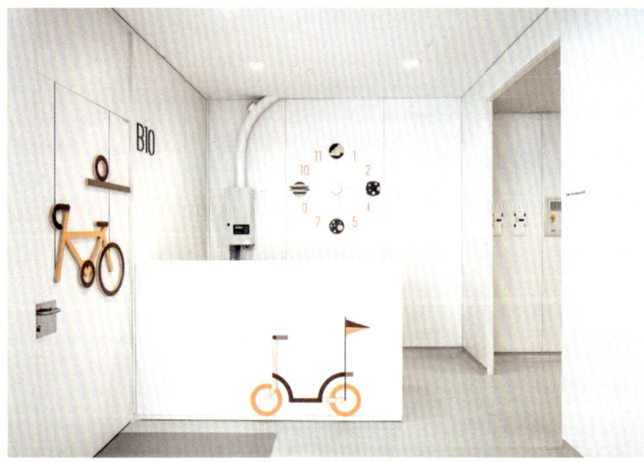
B10

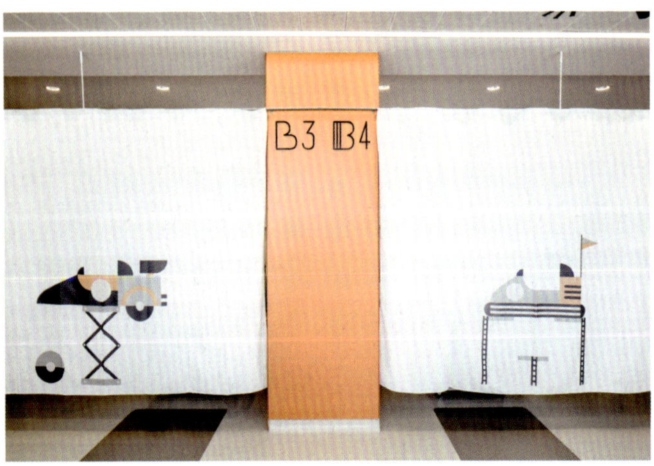
B3 B4

B9

Pirogov's Children Ward

Location: Sofia, Bulgaria

Completion: 2017

Design: FourPlus Studio

Photography: MEM Studio

Awards: Building of the Year Bulgaria, 2017 – Special Prize

This project focuses on transforming the children's ward in Pirogov Hospital to make its patients' stay more pleasant and cheerful through interesting illustrations, visuals and a bilingual navigation system. Three floors underwent a makeover to emerge as a colorful imaginary world with illustrated walls, corridors and rooms. A beautiful, blue ocean with friendly sea creatures engulfs the first floor, splashing across walls in eye-catching illustrations of a giant blue whale, cute dolphins, sealions, calming seascapes, and a serene turtle, among others. Fairytale characters commandeer the second floor and take over the space with captivating gardens, forest animals and princesses. The third floor is a playground for superheroes in their dandy capes who whoosh by on their quests to save the day.

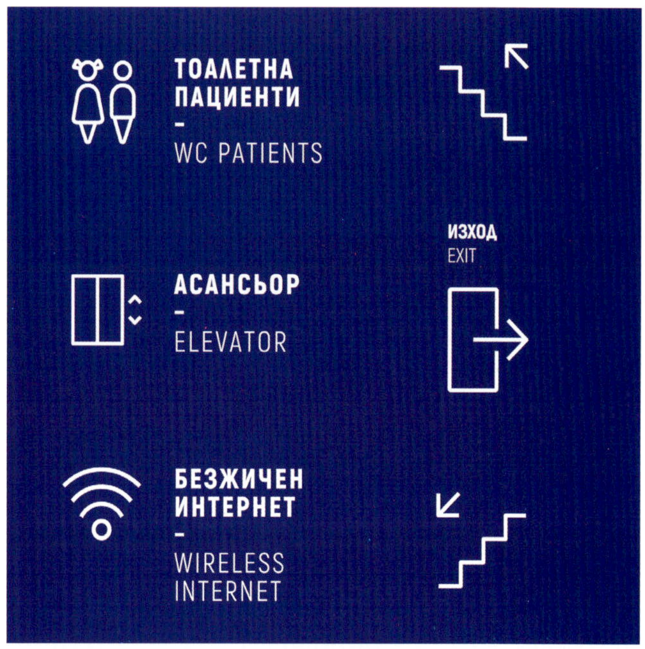

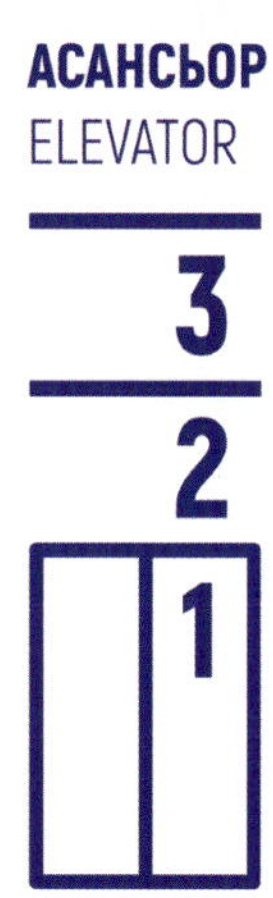

The visual outfits on each floor are tailored to the age group of patients that particular level caters to. As the first floor houses the reception, waiting room and general offices, the visuals are designed to appeal to audiences of all ages. Fairytales are selected for the second floor as it is visited mostly by younger children; the colorful graphics splashed on the walls are visually engaging and act as visual stimuli that draw them into the fairytale world. On the third floor, superheroes that identify with people in the children's lives—supermoms, super-firefighters, super-teachers, and doctors—display their special "super powers." Designed for children between 3 and 18, whom are more conversational, these images are selected to remind them of their close kin and their love and care, encouraging the children to recover and return home to them.

A bilingual navigation system ensures patients and visitors find their way around the hospital without trouble, making the experience as easy as child's play.

ДЕТСКА РЕГИСТРАТУРА
PEDIATRIC RECEPTION
201
и ОПЕРАЦИОННА ЗАЛА
4
ДЕТСКА КОРЕМНА ХИРУРГИЯ
3
ДЕТСКА ТРАВМАТОЛОГИЧНА КЛИНИКА
ХИРУРГИЯ НА НОВОРОДЕНОТО
2
ДЕТСКА ГРЪДНА ХИРУРГИЯ
КОНСУЛТАТИВНИ КАБИНЕТИ
1
CONSULTING ROOMS

111
122
202
208

ЕТАЖ
3
FLOOR
ДЕТСКА КОРЕМНА ХИРУРГИЯ
–
PEDIATRIC ABDOMINAL SURGERY
ЕТАЖ
2
FLOOR
ХИРУРГИЯ НА НОВОРОДЕНОТО
–
NEONATAL SURGERY

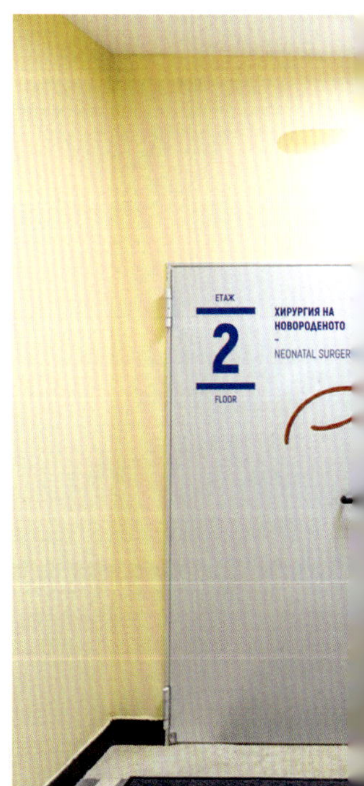
ЕТАЖ
2
FLOOR
ХИРУРГИЯ НА НОВОРОДЕНОТО
–
NEONATAL SURGER

ЕТАЖ
3
FLOOR
ДЕТСКА КОРЕМНА ХИРУРГИЯ
-
PEDIATRIC ABDOMINAL SURGERY

ЕТАЖ
2
FLOOR
ХИРУРГИЯ НА НОВОРОДЕНОТО
-
NEONATAL SURGERY

ДЕТСКА РЕГИСТРАТУРА
-
PEDIATRIC RECEPTION
ДЕТСКИ КОНСУЛТАТИВНИ КАБИНЕТИ
-
PEDIATRIC CONSULTING ROOMS
УНГ
-
OTORHINOLARYNGOLOGY
ОЧЕН КАБИНЕТ
-
OPHTHALMOLOGIST
СЪДОВА ХИРУРГИЯ
-
VASCULAR SURGERY
ОПЕРАТИВНА ГИНЕКОЛОГИЯ
-
OPERATIONAL GYNECOLOGY
ХИРУРГИЯ И ТЕРАПИЯ НА РЪКАТА
-
ARM SURGERY AND THERAPY

4A
СТАЯ
ROOM

4
СТАЯ
ROOM

7
СТАЯ
ROOM

The New Polyclinic

Location: Perm, Russia

Completion: 2018

Design: Ozon Group (Ltd.)

Photography: Alexei Gushchin

This was a large-scale project aimed at renewing more than 100 polyclinics in Perm Krai, Russia to increase the quality of healthcare and improve people's access to it, and at the same time create a friendly and comfortable environment for patients, visitors, and staff.

Key steps included establishing new common access standards, new visual identity guidelines (so each polyclinic project could be managed remotely), improving signage and navigation within polyclinics, and adding a touch of warmth to the austerity of the interior design.

A tailored concept meticulously executes elements in each polyclinic, spanning navigation design, information boards design, colors, illustrations, and 3D design, to set in place two new visual identities—one for the adult-focused polyclinics and the other for the children's polyclinics.

The walls in the children's polyclinics speak through colorful, expressive characters that adorn large murals. In a vibrant variety of scenes, the engaging visuals, which include the ocean, the taiga biome of Perm Krai, jungle animals, and creatures from the Permian period immerse the children's polyclinics in a friendly ambiance that puts children at ease.

In some of the polyclinics, the images that star in the murals are hung from the ceiling as printed artworks, like colorful bunting announcing a warm, children-focused environment. An analysis of direct feedback, as well as that from parents and social media, indicate that the new visuals are well-received and a success. Riding on this positive note, there are plans in the future to animate some of the characters for a children's tutorial on good hygiene practices and daily care routine, such as the importance of brushing one's teeth properly and washing one's hands before eating.

Страховой представитель
Регистратор
Регистратура
Расписание работы врачей-педиатров
Информация

Выход
Информация

Колясочная
Информация

Заборный пункт лаборатории
Отделение профилактических осмотров
WC
Буфет

110 Кабинет «Здоровое детство»
Буфет

Консультативно-диагностическое отделение
2
Лечебно-профилактическое отделение
2

сорока
олень
кабан
Администрация поликлиники
222

LOTOS Children's Clinic

Location: Chelyabinsk, Russia

Completion: 2016

Design: Sasha Sherstneva, Alexey Panov and Inga Habibulina

Photography: Medical Center Lotos

LOTOS Children's Clinic in Chelyabinsk, Russia strives to create a less intimidating experience for children visiting medical facilities. Research conducted among parents and children revealed that children are afraid of doctors in white coats, injections, and the usually unfriendly atmosphere in most clinics and hospitals. In order to overcome these challenges, the design aims to relieve children and parents of stress and turn treatment into a fun game.

This design path arrives at the concept of clinic heroes, made up of three superhero main acts who accompany little patients through their clinic visit. They can be seen carrying out different missions in relation to the specific functions of that particular clinic unit and the pre-empted emotions of the children. For example, in the laboratory, they make a vaccine of courage, and at the hearing specialist, they send out a secret message for the children. These different missions generate great interest and engagement among the children who are curious to see what mission the clinic heroes are on in other areas.

Not only do these superheroes fill the clinic floors, they also front the clinic's visual identity and frame the clinic's corporate identity, appearing on clinic stationery and official documents, such as visit/appointment cards. The visual identity is continued with fun, children-friendly icons that guide navigation within the building and mark out key areas/rooms in the clinic through large door signs. A bright and cheery color palette completes the visual identity, painting waiting areas, treatment rooms and other areas in the clinic in lively doses of lime green, orange, turquoise, and red, among other uplifting shades. To that extent, staff uniforms are also brightly colored instead of white so that children do not form negative associations with doctors, nurses, and other medical staff.

Designed with thought and an understanding of their target market, LOTOS clinic asserts an informal, inviting, and warm visual language to determine a comfortable and non-hostile environment. To create even more positive association through fun and engagement, play stands and distorting mirrors help dispel anxious nerves to pass waiting time with playful distractions.

КЛИНИКА ДЛЯ ДЕТЕЙ
ВИЖУ БЕРЕГ В ОБА ГЛАЗА НЕ НУЖНЫ МНЕ ВОДОЛАЗЫ
ЛОТОС
КЛИНИКА ДЛЯ ДЕТЕЙ
Я СЕГОДНЯ У ВРАЧА ГРОМЧЕ ВСЕХ СКАЗАЛА «А-А-А»
ЗАПИСЬ НА ПРИЕМ
220-00-03
ВЫЗОВ ВРАЧА
КОГДА ЛЕЧЕНИЕ – ПРИКЛЮЧЕНИЕ

ЛОТОС
КЛИНИКА ДЛЯ ДЕТЕЙ
Челябинск, Труда 187-б
www.lotos74.ru
Единая справочная служба:
+7(351) 220 00 03
ЛОТОС
КЛИНИКА ДЛЯ ДЕТЕЙ
• педиатрия
• узкие специалисты • узи
• детский патронаж от рождения до года
• вызов врача на дом

ЛОТОС
МЕДИЦИНСКАЯ КАРТА
ИСТОРИЯ РАЗВИТИЯ РЕБЕНКА

ЛОТОС

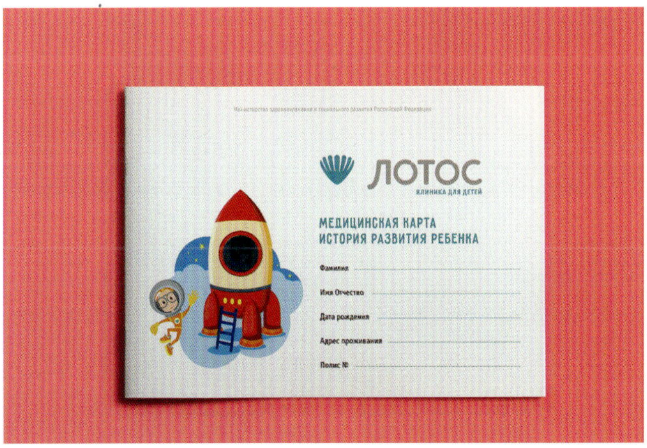
ЛОТОС
КЛИНИКА ДЛЯ ДЕТЕЙ
МЕДИЦИНСКАЯ КАРТА
ИСТОРИЯ РАЗВИТИЯ РЕБЕНКА
Фамилия
Имя Отчество
Дата рождения
Адрес проживания
Полис №

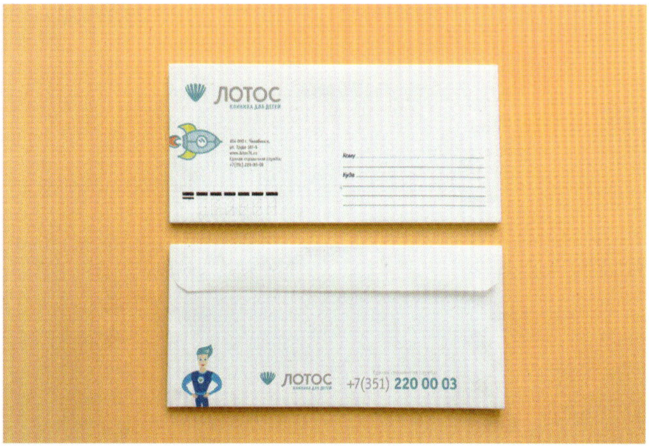
ЛОТОС
КЛИНИКА ДЛЯ ДЕТЕЙ
ЛОТОС
+7(351) 220 00 03

ЛОР
11

КАБИНЕТ УЗИ

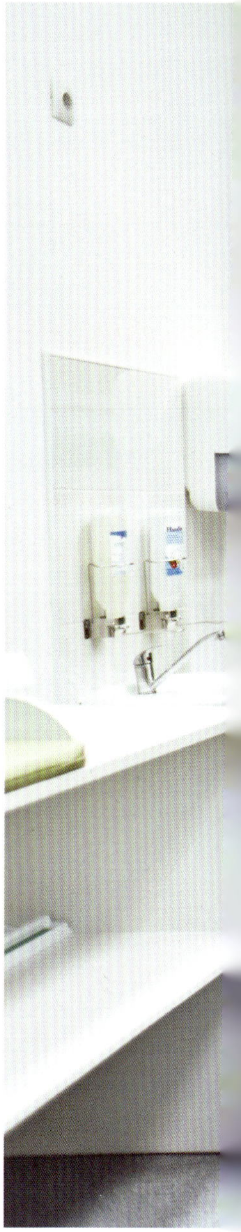

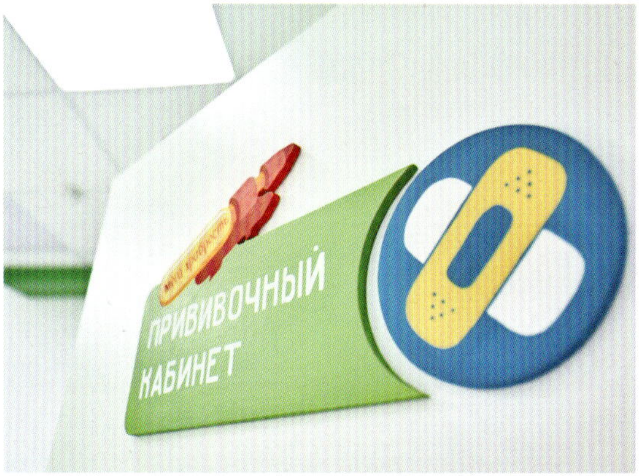
ПРИВИВОЧНЫЙ
КАБИНЕТ

ДЕРМАТОЛОГ

ГАРДЕРОБ
КОЛЯСОЧНАЯ

ПЕДИАТР
6

1
КАБИНЕТ
ИГРОВАЯ
КОМНАТА

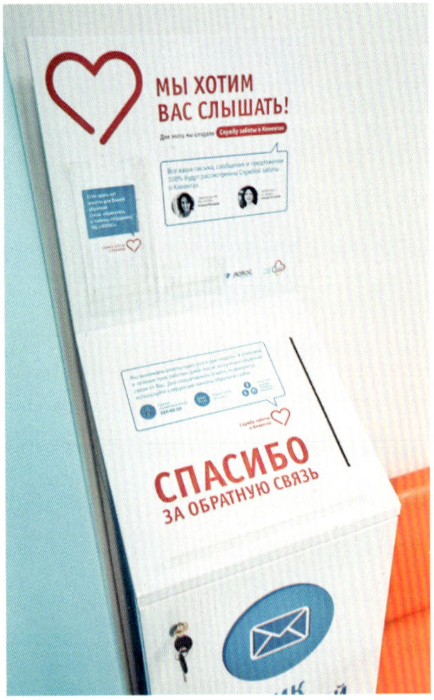
МЫ ХОТИМ
ВАС СЛЫШАТЬ!
СПАСИБО
ЗА ОБРАТНУЮ СВЯЗЬ

ПЕЧАТЬ
ФОТО
#LOTOS74

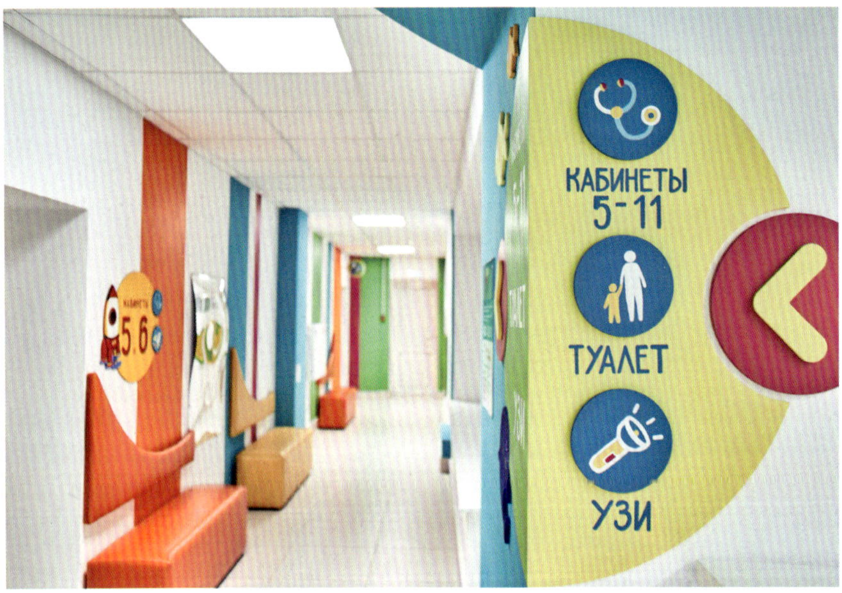
КАБИНЕТЫ
5-11
ТУАЛЕТ
УЗИ

ПРОЦЕДУРНЫЙ
КАБИНЕТ
3
10

КАБИНЕТЫ
1 и 2
10 и 11
ИГРОВАЯ
КОМНАТА
АКУСТИЧЕСКАЯ
КОМНАТА
10

ВЗРОСЛАЯ ПОЛИКЛИНИКА

ПОЙДЁМ
ИГРАТЬ!

НЕВРОЛОГ

РЕГИСТРАТУРА
10

Culture

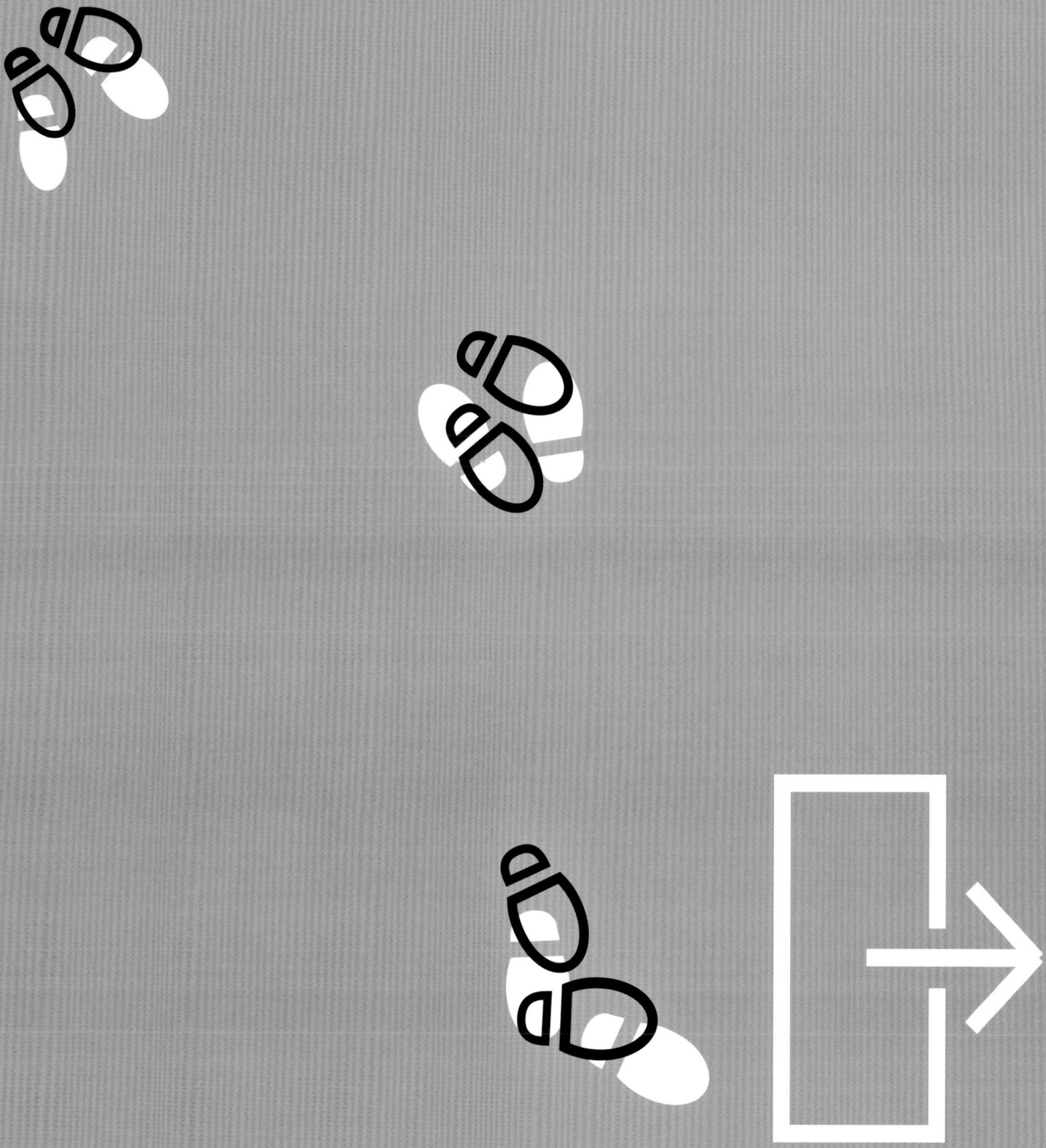

Arirang Public Library for Children

Location: Seoul, Korea

Completion: 2017

Design: form & function

Photography: form & function

Yellow, pink, and sky-blue color each floor of the Arirang Public Library for Children located in Seongbuk-gu, Seoul. Given the depth and strong identity of these colors, as well as their wide application throughout the library, the logo is developed in black and white. The logo is a fun, cartoon-like face with focus on the eyes, which are supposed to represent a child reading a book. It is also an "active" key feature that changes its pupil direction to suit the logo's application.

Children are always observant of interesting things, viewing them with different perspectives from that of an adult; they are constantly curious and always asking "why?" The funny, friendly, logo face stimulates this curiosity and also kindles the fun of reading and learning, and in turn, the joy of visiting the library. The logo also wears a smile, subconsciously impressing the enjoyable activities that the library environment presents; the changing eye directions further reflect the inherent curious nature of a child. The wordmark in Hangeul characters is designed in a larger than normal ratio based on the physical proportions of a child, so that the characters look like life-size pictorials, which amuses the children.

Navigation guides on the floor incorporate the logo and an image of the hill where the library is located. The smiling logo atop the hill reflects a happy child that is growing up enjoying the joys of reading. The repetition of the logo in different variations and on different components outlines a cohesive visual identity.

However, avoiding the saturation of visual identity elements is crucial, especially in a small-scale library such as this. The use of the main logo in as many of the elements as possible gives it prominence and retains the character of the visual identity without overpowering a modest space.

아리랑 어린이 도서관
아리랑어린이도서관
시범운영기간 안내
아리랑어린이도서관
시범운영기간 안내

아리랑 어린이 도서관

아리랑
어린이
도서관
sb 성북
성북문화재단

2F
어린이 열람실
안내데스크
창작마루
생각마루
서로이음 세미나실
북적북적2 동아리실

1F
영유아 열람실
안내데스크
그림책방
노리마루
다가치 자원활동실
맘휴 休
수유공간
북적북적1 동아리실

아리랑 어린이

B1
통합안내
회원가입 | 대출반납

아리랑 어린이도서관
ARIRANG PUBLIC LIBRARY FOR CHILDREN
아리랑어린이도서관
시범운영 기간입니다

검색

Children's Festival: Small Big Dreamers

Location: Singapore

Completion: 2018

Design: WY-TO

Photography: Frank Pinckers

Organized by Singapore National Gallery, the Children's Festival – Small Big Dreamers is part of the gallery's efforts to engage the young and open their minds to new ideas to help them explore creativity and "reimagine the world around them." This first edition led children to discover art through body movement, spotlighting Singapore-based artist Lee Wen, one of the pioneers of performance art in his homeland; the exhibition is a vague homage to Lee Wen's spirited and valiant battle against Parkinson's disease, which limits his movements, yet does little to deter him, as evidenced by his works that convey his sense of optimism.

The visual identity catered to both the overall Children's Festival theme of imagination, as well as the dedicated exhibition theme of movement. It found form in the inspiring installations and colorful, bold visual outfits designed to appeal to children. These visuals spanned displays, exhibition souvenirs—such as the art pack— and marketing collaterals.

The festival logo, which will be maintained through all editions of the Children's Festival employs an artistic and eye-catching typography that visually puns with the words "small" and "big," as it playfully reflects them in contrasting font sizes, creating a strong identity while amusing children by this first display of creativity and artistic flair.

On the exhibition display boards, dynamic characters teamed with creative copy to awaken the imagination as they guided children through the exhibition, encouraging them to lead with their imaginations to form their own unique narratives to experience the journey through the many installations.

In the design of the installations themselves, coordinated actions were key considerations. The interactive installations highlighted narrow pathways, low entryways, and varying-height "obstacles" to encourage movement in order to navigate the space and explore the parameters of the exhibition, creating much excitement and delight for the children. To heighten the sensory stimulation and "experiential art" effect, the exhibition also weaved in a range of active-play discoveries that included coloring, folding paper planes, and making interesting sounds with everyday objects, such as clanging pots with ladles—needless to say, a running favorite among the many children who attended.

To complement the highly stimulating setting and highly interactive stage of the festival, bright colors were employed to instantly attract the attention of children. In order to match the main colors of the exhibition area, orange and blue dressed packaging, the festival logo, and exhibition take-homes like the art pack, which drove home the notion of embracing the imagination to empower one's world.

KEPPEL
CENTRE FOR
ART EDUCATION

LIGHTS, SYMMETRY, REFLECTION!

THE RAINBOW CONCERT HALL MAY GET
NOISY WHEN THERE ARE MORE LITTLE
MUSICIANS AROUND. IF YOU PREFER
QUIETER SPACES, ASK OUR FRIENDLY
GALLERY AMBASSADORS WHERE TO GO.

TAP!!!

GALLERY
CHILDREN'S FESTIVAL
SMALL-BIG DREAMERS
ENTER HERE
9 JUN – 9 SEP 2018
#SMALLBIGDREAMERS

Lee Wen
Sun Path
Mixed media
1830 x 270 cm
When was the last time you watched the sunset?
When Lee Wen was in India for two months in 1992, he watched the sunset every day. The setting sun looked like a giant red ball dominating the skies to him. Lee Wen tried to take a picture of it but found that the camera could not capture its splendour fully. Instead, he performed Journey of a Yellow Man No. 2: The Fire and the Sun as a tribute to these beautiful sunsets that lit up the skies with a spectrum of wondrous colours.
TAKE A CLOSER LOOK AT THE IMAGE OF THE SUN SETTING OVER THE BRIDGE.
DO YOU NOTICE HOLES IN THE IMAGE?
PICK ONE OF THE ROPES ON THE BRIDGE AND LOOP IT THROUGH THESE HOLES. EACH ROPE REPRESENTS A SUNRAY.
DOUBLE THE FUN BY DOING THIS ACTIVITY WITH A FRIEND!

BEGIN YOUR SMALL BIG DREAMERS JOURNEY
Take the escalator at the Padang Atrium to Level 1.
MAKE MUSIC AT THE RAINBOW CONCERT HALL
Venture beyond the rainbow curtain and discover an orchestra of objects to create the perfect soundtrack for your adventures.
STEP INSIDE THE DREAMERS' HAVEN
New journeys can be both exciting and scary. Write your hopes and fears on a pair of wings. Then, leave them behind at the Dreamers' Haven and get ready to charge ahead.
EXPLORE THE ANATOMY OF DREAMERS
Walk through the doors in front of you and enter Anatomy of Dreamers. This space is as bright as the sun. Look out for the Yellow Man on the bridge or under the gazebo of red lanterns. Journey through the obstacles with him.
GET CREATIVE WITH EVERYDAY ITEMS
Find Hands On across the bridge and discover a world of possibilities through simple household items.
THE IMAGINATION CONTINUES
Explore art-inspired spaces and activities at the revamped Keppel Centre for Art Education. Don't forget to leave your name and contact details at the reception desk to receive updates on monthly family programmes!

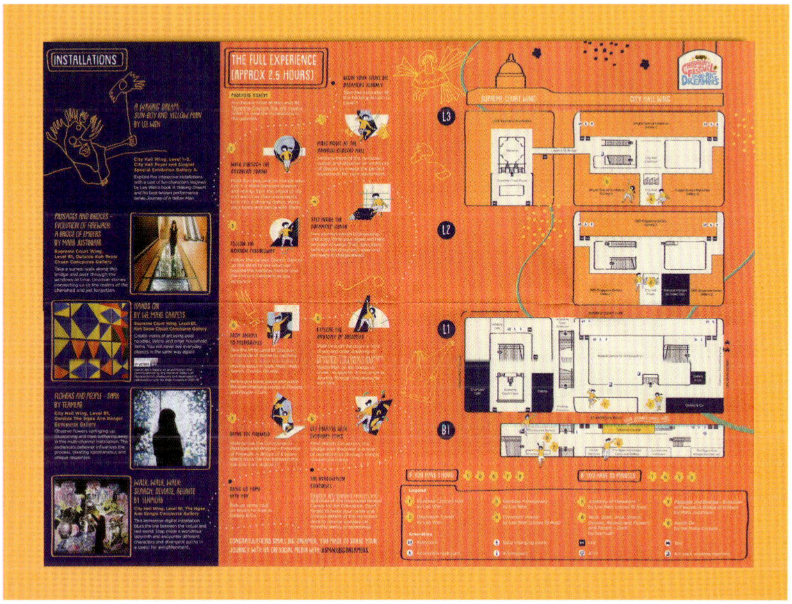
INSTALLATIONS
THE FULL EXPERIENCE (APPROX 2.5 HOURS)
L3
L2
L1
B1

WHO ARE YOU TODAY?
INSTRUCTIONS:

DǒNG DǒNG

Location: Huizhou, China

Completion: 2017

Design: SORA

Photography: Chen Shaocong

DǒNG DǒNG bookstore is designed as an interactive urban space that blends culture, leisure, and education. Through the focal element of books, joined with an inviting interior design and a striking visual identity, the bookstore aspires to encourage knowledge-building and creativity, to expand the worlds of children.

The logo is a combination of a Mandarin and English wordmark finished with a book icon. Both wordmarks are expressed in the same clean font, which features an open character to ensure legibility and ease of recognition. The "o"s in "DONG" are presented with letter accents that reflect an open book, hinting at a playful, creative personality, while creating a strong visual identity that ties in with the brand's book business. Shelf labels employ the same typeface of the Mandarin wordmark to maintain a unified visual identity that is sturdy and undiluted.

Abstract animal graphics add to the mix and complement the space with colorful scenes that depict artistic renditions of the animals and their environments. These unusual graphics stimulate imaginations and nudge children to explore non-archetypical methods and concepts in their day-to-day, and even take on artistic pursuits that uncover their creative side.

A natural timber décor creates an inviting interior that is relaxing and conducive for browsing. Three floors arrange a creative assembly of reading nooks and perches that are unlike a traditional bookstore. A small reading mezzanine and a dedicated picture book zone tailored for younger customers and their parents are among the variety of reading spaces where children can lose themselves in the pages of a book. The Dream College on the third floor provides a space to conduct talks, host classes, and organize movie days. Through an enriching environment coupled with a distinctive visual identity, the bookstore becomes a part of lives and the society at large, making a positive impact in the development of young minds.

董懂 DONG
DONG

DONG DONG

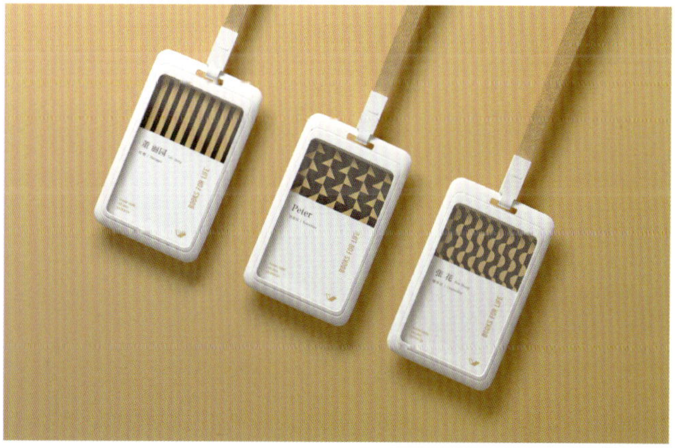
Peter

董懂 DONG DONG

DONG DONG
DONG DONG

少儿读物
艺术 / 摄影
进口书籍
CHILDREN
ART & PHOTOGRAPHY
IMPORT

人文社科
Human Science

BOOKS FOR LIFE
CEYLON

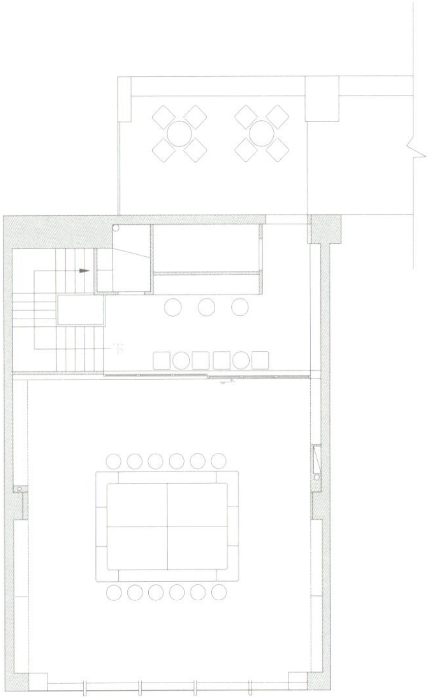

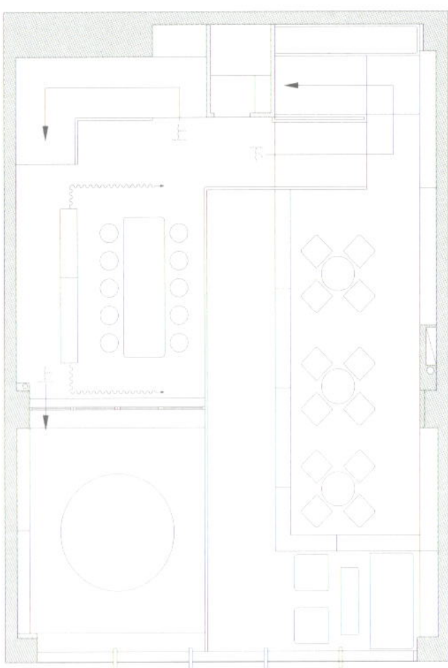

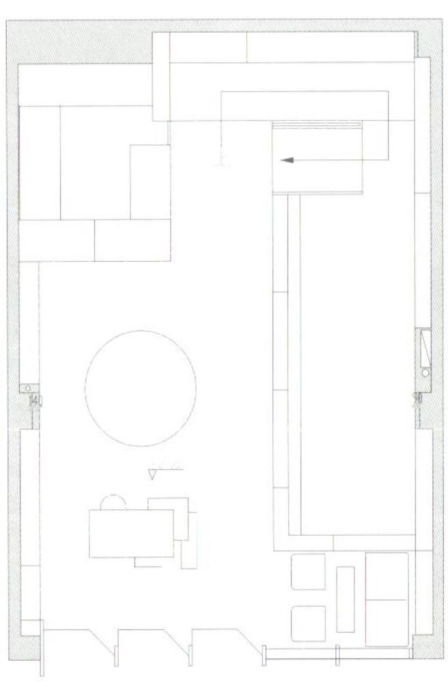

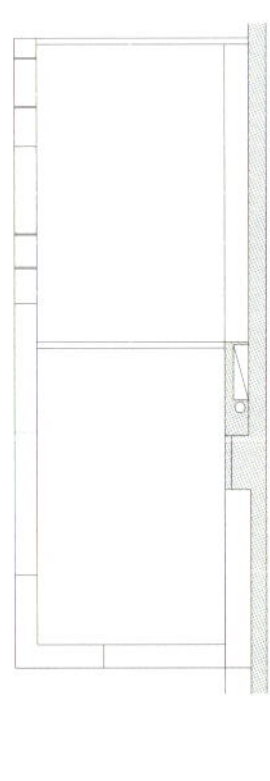

禁止攀爬 | NO CLIMBING

Stand IVAJ

Location: Valencia, Spain

Completion: 2017

Design: Nueve

Photography: David M. Cordón

Institut Valencià de la Joventut (IVAJ) is the agency responsible for coordinating youth policy in the Valencian community. (Its key functions include defending the freedom and social rights of young people, promoting youth participation and support for their structures, and prompting youth services, such as educational leisure activities.) During the Christmas holidays in 2017, IVAJ held two different fairs in Alicante and Valencia offering leisure activities and training for children. Event stands for both carnivals were designed according to the space requirements of the program's activities, and adapted to the site layout.

Conceptualized around the idea of "social diversity," the stand was divided into two different zones, aligned with the event program. The first zone was dedicated to handicrafts, with three large tables, and the second one was designed as an open space, which doubled as a reception area and activity space for other items in the event program.

Graphic motifs representing different cultures around the world were either printed on veneered panels directly, or applied on vinyl. Specifically designed elements created an environment filled with colorful and educational images that embodied the concept, while supporting the function of the stands. Buzzing with lively chatter, knowledge exchange on world cultures, and learning opportunities weaved into fun activities, the occasion, enhanced by the visual treatments, appropriately captured IVAJ's brand personality and qualifies as one for the books.

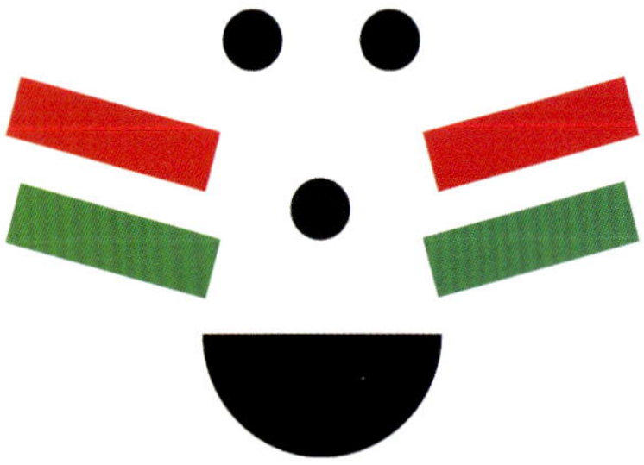

LEVANTE

DIPUTACIÓ DE VALÈNCIA
DIPUTACIÓ DE
VALÈNCIA
Joventut, Esports i Igualtat
B
2
Joventut

Retail

Bin&Bông Shop

Location: Hanoi, Vietnam

Completion: 2018

Design: Luong Hiep

Photography: 3003 studio

Bin&Bông is a store for babies and moms started by a mother with two young children. The store is set in a typical Vietnamese tube house, over two floors measuring 10,764 square feet (1,000 square meters) each, and branded with a fun and catchy name that is a creative derivation of the owner's children's names. Basic geometric shapes, such as triangles, squares and circles, similar to the shape of the toys babies play with, are used as accents to create relatability for the children who accompany their mothers to the shop.

The interior colors range in gentle pastel tones that are delicate but noticeable, and include schemes of baby-blue and pink that accent white backgrounds. This mild color palette, usually associated with mothers and babies, creates a cozy and friendly ambiance that identifies with mothers and children alike, while anchoring the shop's visual identity. In line with its slogan "make mom's life easy," the store showcases fixed display shelves alongside merchandise counters on castors, which can be moved around and rearranged as pleased, awarding flexibility to the space. Display units are simple and easy to handle: removable steel frames form hanging racks that can be conveniently set-up and dismantled as needed, and rolling cabinets allow opportunities to tailor the space according to seasonal and festive themes. With a varying décor that creates always-interesting shopping experiences, the shop is an ideal venue for a family-fun afternoon shopping spree.

KID
2 year To 5 year
S
XXL

XL

B&B
Milk
children's

Kidsmoment

Location: Wuhan, China

Completion: 2016

Design: RIGI

Photography: Yue Ping

The design of Kidsmoment children's clothing shop begins with substantial research on clothing design for children and the shopping behavior associated with children's apparel. As it is usually parents that undertake and dictate the activity of shopping, it can be said that the retail success of children's clothing is based on an unseen social relationship, first and foremost, with parents.

Tailored around the anchor word "trust"— the trust forged between the shop and parents making the purchase—the interior design is clean, light, and buoyant. By increasing display efficiency and controlling the color, materials, and design of display shelves, an attractive and comfortable retail space is fashioned through a thoughtfully presented visual identity.

A VIP zone and a kids' experience zone are strategically implemented to increase customer loyalty and children engagement, respectively. The VIP zone promotes product deals catered exclusively for VIP customers, while in selected nooks, interesting and fun elements are incorporated to keep children engaged. A measuring wall makes for an entertaining time as children have fun indulging in silly antics to capture a "taller" or "shorter" height reading. A blackboard wall calls out to the more creative of the lot who contentedly while away the moments with expressive doodles.

To build a sincere connection with customers, it is essential to walk in the customers' shoes. Understanding parents' appreciation of a safe environment for their children, all hard edges of furniture are chamfered. The children's perspectives are also considered, and to that end, the design splashes geometrical graphics all over the shop, from fixtures to feature walls, to point of purchase locations, to create the ambiance of being at home with familiar toys.

As children are also sensitive to numbers, large numerals are printed on selected conspicuous areas to outline and enhance the spatial order of zoning. Illustrations are also widely used in the space together with a series of simple signs that can be easily understood by children; all in all, the visual identity nuances a familiar, comfortable language that resonates with parents as it does children, speaking of fun, care, sincerity, and most importantly, trust.

Kidsmoment

Kidsmoment
KIDS
MOMENT

2
2
KIDSM
BOY&GI
MEMB

2015
KIDSMOMENT
BOY&GIRL
NEW LOOK

5
KIDSMOMENT
NEW LOOK

THE FUNNY
MOMENTS
OF DISCOVERY
KIDSMOMENT
MEMBER ZONE
2
KIDSMOMENT
MEMBER ZONE
KM

2
4

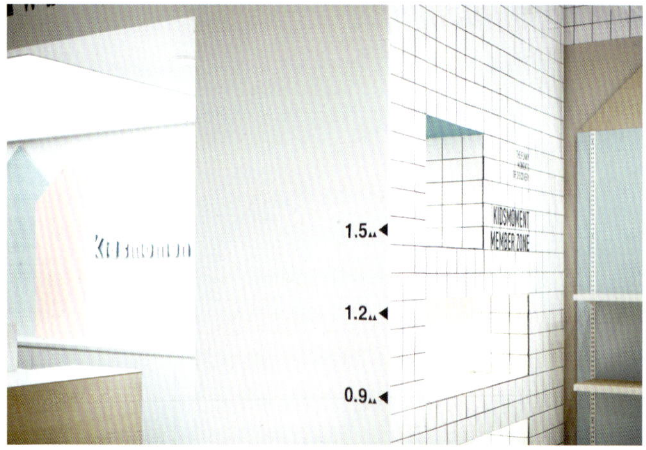
1.5
1.2
0.9
KIDSMOMENT
MEMBER ZONE

6
KIDSMOMENT
NEW LOOK

KIDSIDEA
1.5
1.2
0.9

FITTING
ROOM
6
NEW LOOK

3
KIDS
WORLD

2
4
4
KIDSMOMENT
BOY&GIRL
NEW LOOK

Kindo

Location: San Pedro Garza García, Mexico

Completion: 2015

Design: Anagrama Studio

Photography: Caroga Foto

Kindo is an exclusive boutique that retails children's clothing and accessories in San Pedro Garza García, Mexico. The store offers a wide selection of original clothing items for children.

The brand identity is formed along a didactic bead maze intercepted and accented by random geometric shapes, which allows fun adaptations with a twist in the store design. The color palette reflects a child's energetic and open personality with a wide range of pastel and neon tones that team with a logo that embodies the interesting mix of classic and new that make up the brand personality.

The interior layout aims to create an enjoyable and engaging experience for both adults and children through a dynamic space that utilizes parts of the maze for product display. The tubes of the maze function as clothing display racks and the beads present "shelves" to exhibit accessories. The visual identity of the boutique's interior complements the brand's corporate identity while also designing the shop as a unique space. Better than that, it also creates an inviting atmosphere that suggests an enjoyable shopping experience.

KINDO

KINDO
SHOP
FOR THE LITTLE ONES

KINDO
SHOP
FOR THE LITTLE ONES

KINDO
SHOP
FOR THE LITTLE ONES

KINDO
KINDO

KINDO
KINDO
KINDO
KINDO

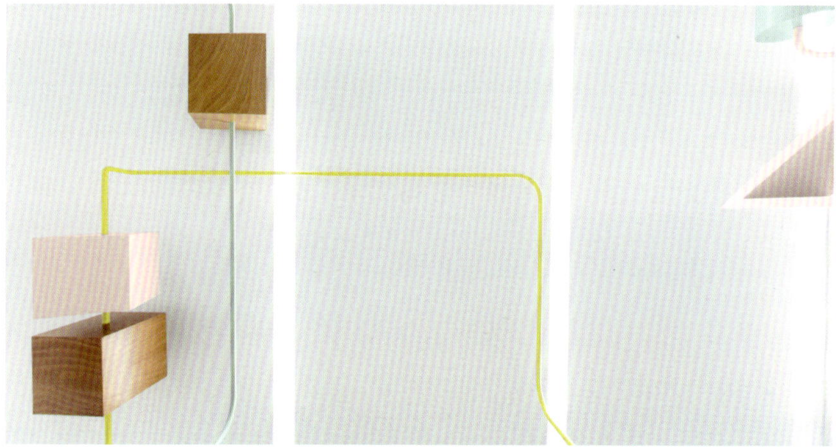

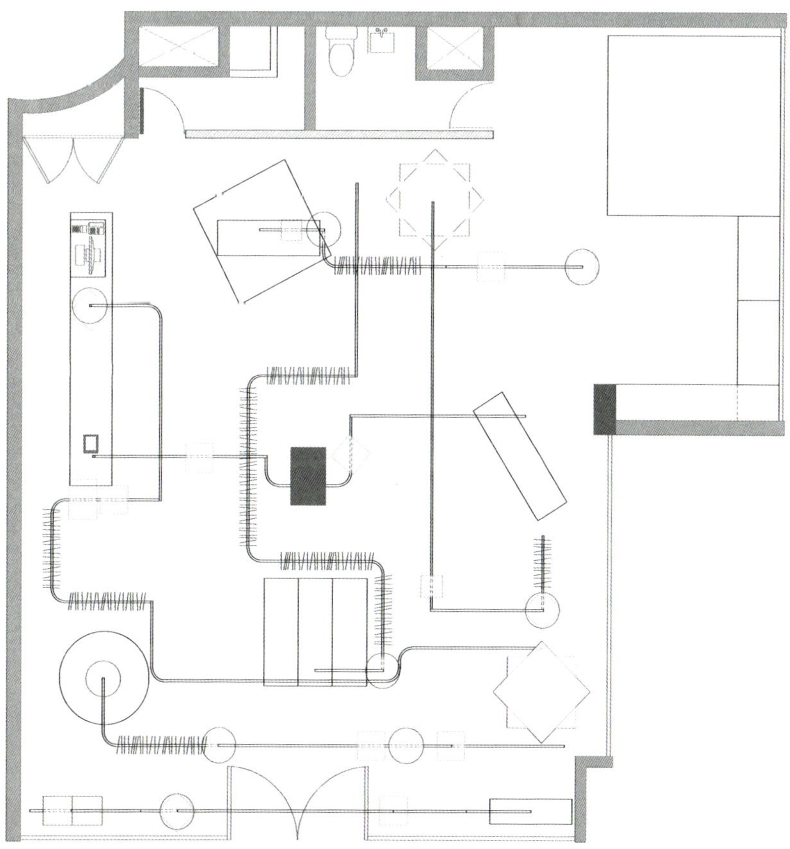

Little Stories

Location: Valencia, Spain

Completion: 2018

Design: Clap Studio

Photography: Daniel Rueda

Little Stories is a concept store that retails shoes exclusively for children. Designed with a strong visual identity, the interior is based on the three key points that form the essence of Little Stories: game, simplicity, and adaptability.

A wordmark in simple sans serif typography frames the visual identity and it is completed with line doodles to articulate the brand logo. To create a one-of-a-kind experience for little ones that visit the store, the design and décor are tailored to encourage imagination and play while appropriately showcasing merchandise. They also map out a cohesive visual identity by repeating the fun, squiggly doodles in the logo in a variety of patterns throughout the interior.

An open layout, which features large windows and a central column creates the illusion of an extraordinarily large interior that appears more like a gallery than a shop. Small, movable floor stands and wall-mounted magnetic metal plates allow flexible and adaptable product displays that can be easily updated to keep the décor dynamic.

The visual identity of Little Stories announces itself right at the outset with a storefront that prominently displays the brand name and the light-hearted logo imagery. Tasked to create brand association and catch attention, these visual elements also put a friendly, playful face forward that children can relate to and identify with. This playful character extends to the interior with cylinders that "grow" out of the ceiling. Housing light points, they illuminate the space and the products, drawing children's focus to merchandise on display. This group effort of many fun and out-of-the-world elements dazzle children with a captivating space that makes a joyful game of shoe-shopping.

Little Stories

Little Stories
Little Stories

Little Stories

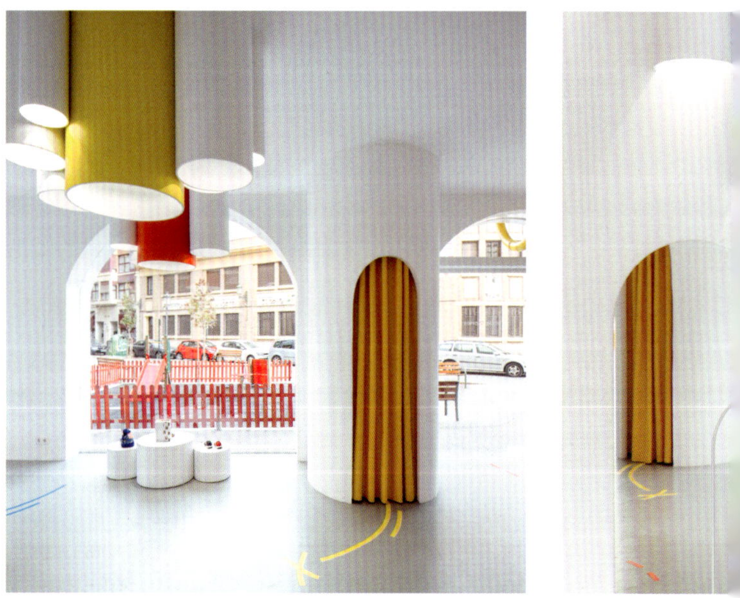

Little Stories
www.littlestories.es

Little Stories
www.littlestories.es
+34 963 445 075
hello@littlestories.es
Facebook-Instagram:
@littlestories.es

Little Stories

Little Stories

Maui Popsicle

Location: Hawaii, USA

Completion: 2017

Design: Brandon Archibald

Photography: Brandon Archibald

Maui Popsicle, which was to be located in Maui Harbor Shopping Center, Maui Island, Hawaii, was a project initiated in 2017 by the development company USAI Investments in Dallas, Texas, but for various reasons, was not realised beyond its concept stage.

The focus of this project was to develop a brand concept, supporting visual identity and the interior design of the first outlet in the chain.

The tiki, an icon in Polynesian culture, referring to different types of humanoid carvings or idols used in sacred Maori ceremonies was selected as the branding element. Paying homage to its deep roots in Hawaiian culture and its widespread association, an icon of a tiki with a popsicle in hand was created as a logo. Together, the tiki and the popsicle speak plainly of the brand and its business, and just in case consumers have trouble "cracking the code," a playful and attractive wordmark of the brand reins in the message with a popsicle in place of the "o" in "Maui Pops."

A mixture of contemporary motifs and a vivacious color palette, characteristic of the Hawaiian spirit, set the tone for the interior design. The logo is featured in the shop interior as well, and welcomes customers with the promise of something cold, refreshing and delicious. Images of juicy fruits affirm that promise by indicating the variety of popsicle flavors available. A uniquely shaped counter adds dynamism to the visual language and hints at the brand's wacky character. Chairs in three different height variations ensure that every customer (toddlers, children, and adults) has a comfortable seat that is just right for that perfect pop of "chill."

maui POPS

Aloha nui loa
GIFT SHOP
maui pops

MANGO TANGO
HANA HOU
LANI KAI
FIGGIN AWESOME
AKAMAI

maui pops
maui pops

TO DO
LIST
WASH dishes
buy A cake
plan VACATION
order pizza
At 3 p.m.

maui
POPS
maui
POPS

maui pops
TIKI BOOM
ALOHA!
&6 89
* + =

HERE YOU CAN TASTE DELICIOUS
maui pops
MADE
OF NATURAL INGREDIENTS THAT GROW UNDER
BRIGHT HAWAIIAN
AS FOR
HE LIKES
AND POPSICLE THE MOST
ALOHA

maui pops

maui pops
maui pops

THE
maui

TIKI
BOOM
maui
POPS

maui
POPS
TIKI
BOOM

Petit Boo – Baby & Kids

Location: Porto, Portugal

Completion: 2015

Design: Axon Studio

Photography: Álvaro Martino

Petit Boo – Baby & Kids is a concept store focused on children and retails an enormous variety of products of more than 30 brands to accompany a little one from "baby" to "child."

The project began with creating a distinct name, later followed by branding and communications media, including a graphic line, client cards, gift bags, and merchandising elements. The design of all branding materials is tuned to reflect a brand image that represents fun, zero gender distinction, cheerfulness, and a smidge of practicality to tie it all together. Yellow, one of the brightest and most energetic colors, commands the visual identity and conveys the positive traits of clarity, optimism, warmth, joy, positivity, and radiance—well suited for a brand that centers on children.

To create more brand awareness and tap into a wider, global consumer market, the brand also maintains a digital presence and an e-commerce platform to retail its merchandise online. Back-end algorithms, website elements (shopping cart/checkout process and call to action prompts), as well as integrations and automations are thoughtfully and painstakingly coordinated to result in a competent online store that can market the brand's wide variety of products without breaking into a sweat. The online store echoes the visual identity of the retail outlet through colors, with website buttons in the same hue of yellow.

A carefully crafted brand/visual identity impresses Petit Boo as a happy and fun place that is a respite from quotidian, sending children into a world of fantasy, trying on clothes, browsing stationary, or simply just taking in the many delightful items that fill this space of wonder.

Petit Boo
BABY & KIDS

Petit Boo
Petit Boo
Petit Boo
Petit Boo
PETITBOO.PT
WWW.PETITBOO.PT

BABY & KIDS
Petit Boo
C.C. DOLCE VITA, LOJA 1118/C · 4350 414 PORTO, PT
T (351) 223 259 055 · E GERAL@PETITBOO.PT
WWW.PETITBOO.PT
Petit Boo
Petit Boo

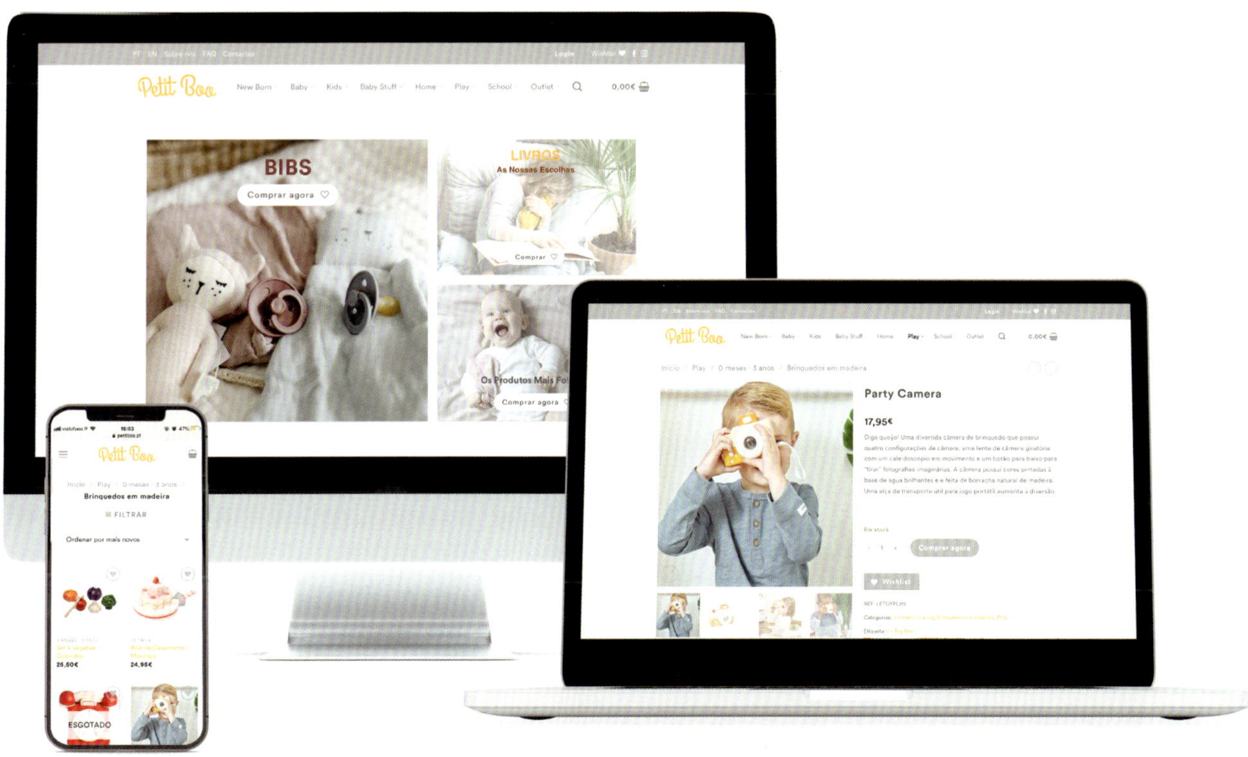
Petit Boo
New Born
Baby
Kids
Baby Stuff
Home
Play
School
Outlet
0,00€
BIBS
Comprar agora
LIVROS
As Nossas Escolhas
Comprar
Os Produtos Mais Fo
Comprar agora
Petit Boo
Party Camera
17,95€
Comprar agora
Wishlist
Petit Boo
Brinquedos em madeira
FILTRAR
Ordenar por mais novos
25,50€
24,95€
ESGOTADO

Petit Boo
BABY & KIDS

Petit Boo
BABY & KIDS
C.C. DOLCE VITA PORTO
WWW.PETITBOO.PT
Petit Boo
Petit Boo
Petit Boo
Petit Boo

Petit Roy

Location: Saint-Jean-sur-Richelieu, Canada

Completion: 2016

Design: Taktik design

Photography: Maxime Brouillet

Chaussures Pierre Roy, a shoe store established in Quebec, Canada in 1972 marked its long-established business with the addition of a new children's store, Petit Roy. Planned around a stimulating and fun concept, the visual design creates engaging and memorable experiences that are as much for the parent as they are for the child. The interior is organized in zones that are tailored for different age groups; each zone is specifically designed to appeal to its target group based on the instinctual behavior of a child at that particular age range.

At the entrance, a wooden hut displaying toddlers' shoes introduces the whimsical visual language of the store design and whisks customers into the Petit Roy fantasy world. The layout in this zone is enclosed, ensuring parents can shop in peace with their infant, free from accidental jostles by excited children. The shoes are also conveniently placed at eye level for easy browsing.

The toddlers' section features mushroom-shaped seats that serve dual purpose: they provide a rush of excitement for young children who enjoy the novelty of feeling taller, sitting on a higher than usual seat, and they make the work of the staff easier, especially when putting on footwear and clothes for the little ones. A tunnel (also the foot/shoe mirror) and a carpet with different size footprints complete the fun menu; as children busy themselves matching their feet to the footprints to figure out their shoe size, they enjoy an engaging and learning experience.

The adults' nook is a relaxed environment with a long bench that prompts parents off their feet for a wee rest. The wooden wall is both a display and a barricade that distances the adjacent hyperactive world of children. Teens also enjoy a specially tailored ambiance, which is set through carefully selected visual outfits; interchangeable pegboard displays break away from the more children-based design elements to add a touch of "cool" that is more relatable and appealing to teens.

When children get restless, a playground at the back of the shop distracts them with a custom-created forest campfire set-up, complete with turf flooring and hanging swings, so parents can finish their shopping without hassle. The visual identity of Petit Roy is holistically crafted to reflect the Petit Roy universe at every angle, even on the outside. Animals from the Quebec forest gather on the shop windows to welcome visitors into the unique world of Petit Roy that is unlike any other, hinting at unbridled fun.

Petit Roy

Petit Roy

Partons à
L'AVENTURE!
Petit Roy
Certificat Cadeau

Petit Roy

Avec ces chaussures,
tu pourras
Pour
De

Petit Roy
www.chaussurespetitroy.com
Petit Roy
www.chaussurespetitroy.com

Petit Roy

Petit Roy
chaussures pour enfants
info@chaussurespetitroy.com
450.346.9849
chaussurespetitroy.com
244, rue Richelieu
Saint-Jean-sur-Richelieu
Québec, Canada, J3B 6X8

Pica Pica Concept Store

Location: Xanthi, Greece

Completion: 2018

Design: we are two

Photography: Grigoris Leontiadis and we are two

PICA PICA Concept Store is a shop and café designed in a playful space that encourages the socialization and creativity of children, while fostering a close relationship with their parents. In a fresh and colorful shop interior, Pica Pica retails furniture, elegant home décor, baby gifts, games, and playful accessories for children.

The name "Pica Pica" is the Latin word for magpie; the namesake is selected for its playful, smart, and inventive nature. "Pica Pica" also draws reference to the word *piccolo*, which means "small" in Italian. The name is playful and unique with a quirky ring to it, making it easy to recall and remember for both children and parents.

The colorful and customizable corporate identity highlights the brand's primary focus on children. The wordmark is inspired by the children's game of wooden bricks—a symbol of creativity and discover in their young years—and presented in a four-color palette. Accompanied by the magpie logo, this visual marks all applications and communicates easily with children as they form a familiar association with the brick imagery. Visual elements and graphics in the venue are also based on the brick form, tailoring a consistent and cohesive visual identity that is easily understood by children.

PiCA PiCA
concept store

PiCA
PiCA
concept store

HAPPY b-DAY
DREAM biG
STAND TALL
HAVE FUN

PiKA PiKA

home
MADE
STAND
TALL

PICAPICA
ENJOY

PiCA PiCA
concept store

the swing
the swing

HAVE FUN
HAPPY B-DAY
STAND TALL
DREAM BIG
MEOW
STAY WILD
HELLO SUN SHINE
HAPPY B-DAY

ΓΝΩΡΙΜΙΑ ΜΕ ΤΟ ΒΙΒΛΙΟ
Δευτέρα 19/3
Ώρα 17:30
στον 1° όροφο
3-6 ετών
PiCA PiCA
concept store

PRICE LIST
PICA PICA
concept store

Pie Pie Kids

Location: Odessa, Ukraine

Completion: 2017

Design: Taisiia Lavrova

Photography: Nikita Lagutin

Pie Pie Kids, a children's clothing and decoration store is built around the following core concept: "a sensitive sense of style and creativity from the earliest years of life." This direction is inspired by the outlook that children should observe nature and grow up in an aesthetic environment, so that they may be nurtured into artists that create beauty for the world.

To embody and reflect this concept, and by extension the inspiration behind it, the interior is special and unusual. Abstract wall murals which successfully align the visual image with the concept are the stars of the space. In waves of colors, they lend an attractive and inspirational accent to the shop's interior, while also firming the corporate identity of the brand.

The murals trail across the shop walls in explosions of random designs and gather the details of the store within a mesmerizing disarray of brushstrokes, smudges and streaks. Through the clever application of color contrast (pastel with bright) and size variations (big on some walls, small on others), this visual outfit evokes a sense of joyful lightness, movement, and playfulness. Incorporating graphic details that include wispy swirls and whooshing lines, the murals scamper from wall to wall and draw attention to interesting store fixtures, such as the house-shaped fitting room, while also presenting product displays against colorful backdrops. Sometimes, they peek out from behind shelves inviting gleeful laughs from children as they entice their imaginations.

The color focus of the murals is a meditative blue, bright yellow, and sweet powder-pink. Brown also plays a part, adding graphical dimension, while grounding the color scheme. Through this delightful collision of colors and visual textures, the artist skilfully captures a child's perception of the world and the auras of freedom, simplicity, and sincerity attached to it.

Store packaging and other printed material repeat the designs of the murals to outline a consistent and connected brand identity.

PiE PiE
kids

PiE PiE
kids

PiE PiE
магазин детской одежды и декора
Каждая вещица в магазине Pie Pie kids — в самое сердце! Со всего мира мы собрали стильные и необычные бренды с историей. Предметы интерьера для детской комнаты датского дизайна, французкая обувь для маленьких аристократов, повседневные костюмчики из самых приятных тканей, нарядные платья любимых европейских и американских брендов!
Все бренды представлены в Pie Pie kids эксклюзивно.
Окружаем эстетикой с детства
PiE PiE
kids
@piepiekids
г. Одесса, ул. Екатерининская, 27
ТЦ «Kadorr», 5 этаж
(093) 550 63 32
· магазин детской одежды и декора ·
PiE PiE
окружаем эстетикой с детства

SUN baby
IZIPIZI

до -40%
SALE
до -40% на одежду и обувь
до -20% на посуду и декор

-40%

SALE

ПРИГЛАШЕНИЕ
-10%

PiF PiF

IZIPIZI

I believe in fairies

PiE PiE
accessorizes
E PiE
cessorizes

PiE PiE
kids
@piepiekids
магазин детской одежды и декора

I believe in fairies
TATTOOS

I believe in fairies
TATTOOS

Index

Ozon Group (Ltd.)
P136
babashorika@gmail.com

Politanski Brand Design
P84
www.pbd.pl

Project M Plus
P94
www.projectmplus.com

Puro Diseño
P74
www.purodiseno.rocks

RIGI
P178
www.rigi-design.com

Sägenvier DesignKommunikation
PP36, 78
www.saegenvier.at

Sasha Sherstneva
P140
dsnalex@gmail.com

Sentido Arquitectura
P50
www.sentidoarquitectura.com

Sid Lee
P120
www.sidlee.com

SORA
P162
www.sorabrand.com

Taisiia Lavrova
P224
tiu.miu.piu@gmail.com

Taktik design
PP66, 210
www.taktikdesign.com

Toormix
P124
www.toormix.com

Vladimir Trinos
P102
www.behance.net/trinosv

we are two
P218
www.wearetwo.gr

WY-TO
P152
www.wy-to.com